RAISING
WILD BIRDS

RAISING WILD BIRDS

LORRAINE PANNETIER

THE UNBOUND PRESS

ISBN 978-1-916529-25-0 Paperback
ISBN 978-1-916529-26-7 Ebook

The Unbound Press
www.theunboundpress.com

Hey unbound one!

Welcome to this magical book brought to you by The Unbound Press.

At The Unbound Press we believe that when women write freely from the fullest expression of who they are, it can't help but activate a feeling of deep connection and transformation in others. When we come together, we become more and we're changing the world, one book at a time!

This book has been carefully crafted by both the contributors and publisher with the intention of inspiring you to move ever more deeply into who you truly are.

We hope that this book helps you to connect with your Unbound Self and that you feel called to pass it on to others who want to live a more fully expressed life.

With much love,
Nicola Humber

Founder of The Unbound Press

www.theunboundpress.com

To my daughters, Nadège and Ayiana,

Thank you for loving me so deeply, forever indulging my love of planes, travel and dance music, and for being such beautiful, amazing, intuitive, kind and gifted human beings.

I love you forever and ever, to infinity and beyond xx

THANK YOU FOR BEING HERE

Before we dive in, let's take a moment together to pause, take a few deep breaths and reconnect to the light that lives within us all…

A visualisation to activate the senses

You're sitting in a park on an old wooden bench in the dappled shade of the trees. As the summer sun touches your bare arms, you begin to imagine the stories, laughter and conversations that have been shared on this seat. That first electric teenage kiss, a mother's warm embrace, the elderly widow pausing to watch the children playing, the young couple drinking takeaway coffee on their way to collect the keys to their first home.

The warm summer breeze brushes through the leaves, creating a soothing sound that lulls you into a peaceful state of mind. Your body visibly relaxes. You pause to take a deeper breath and close your eyes for a few seconds.

A couple of little sparrows fly just above your head, happily tweeting as they flap towards the next chatter stop. Your eyes drift to the lavender bushes in the flower bed, overflowing with an abundance of tiny purple flowers and animated bumble bees collecting pollen, buzzing from one stem to the next. In the distance, three young children are running around, squealing in delight as they splash each other with water from the fountain.

You smile on the inside, not realising you're also beaming radiantly from the outside. An elderly couple walk past and say hello, holding hands as they totter slowly along. A lifetime of togetherness; an unbreakable bond forged from decades of challenges and shared experiences.

The scent of warm honeysuckle floats on the air as a pair of orange and red patterned butterflies flutter in front of you, dancing in the air like graceful ballerinas. In the sky, two planes fly high above, their delicate white trails forming a kiss in the bright blue summer sky.

Feeling blessed to be so deeply immersed in nature, your senses alive and awakened, you close your eyes and tune in even more to the sounds around you. The gentle hum of traffic in the distance, seagulls calling above the sea beyond the town, the bleeping of the pedestrian crossing, a child asking its parent for an ice cream.

The sun dips behind a dainty cloud for a second and the coolness is obvious on your arms. Your hand reaches out to touch the arm of the bench and you realise the metal is hot. You become aware of the wooden bench slats beneath your legs and the breeze gently caressing your shins.

A feeling of sheer pleasure and joy in the moment rises from deep within your belly. Another smile washes over your face as you open your eyes and refocus on the vibrant colours and shapes all around.

You slip off your shoes and begin to walk barefoot across the grass, smiling as you bounce through patches of springy clover, content with twenty minutes of reconnection to Mother Nature and to your inner child before getting back on with your day.

CONTENTS

Part One: The Baby Bird

Part Two: Learning To Fly

Part Three: Soaring High

PROLOGUE

If you found a fragile, injured bird, you'd naturally want to help. The compassion and kindness that live within every human soul would override everything else you were planning to do in that moment to take care of this helpless creature. Depending on the type of bird and its injuries, you may take it straight to a veterinary care centre for the experts to work their magic, or you might take it home, create a special box 'home' for it in a warm, safe place and go out of your way to buy puréed cat food (even if you don't have a cat!) and a pipette to help it drink.

While on one hand this injured creature is weak and helpless, you inherently know that it has an inner strength to fight and an instinct to survive. You'll do everything in your power to help it live, so that it can grow into a big, strong adult bird and thrive in its natural environment; soaring high above treetops, mountains and oceans.

How do you love and care for a baby bird?

You make it feel safe. You hold it close. You let it feel your warmth, love and presence. You nourish it with food and water. You make its surroundings comfortable, secure and warm.

You might spend time holding the little bird, talking to it and willing it to live, saying things like 'Come on little one, you can do it, just eat the food, yes, yes like that!'. You would no doubt feel a sense of motherly love in some way, using your innate, intuitive human traits of compassion, love and nurture to help the bird regain its strength and go on to thrive in its natural habitat.

Of course, you'd never deliberately hurt the baby bird. You wouldn't criticise it for being helpless. You wouldn't tell it it was weak, pathetic or bad for being injured. You wouldn't get angry with it, nor leave it in the dark, alone, with no food or water.

So, why is it then, that we perceive our own weakness as a bad thing and continuously berate ourselves for not being enough?

Why do we, as humans in Western cultures, perceive those with different emotional and mental health situations as weak or different or 'less' in some way? Why do we judge ourselves and others with so much anger, resentment and negativity?

Why is it so difficult to treat ourselves with the same level of consistent love, kindness, compassion, nurture and nourishment that we would give to an injured young bird or animal?

This is a story of Love versus Fear.

A story that highlights many of the ways we exist on planet Earth when fear is the dominant energy, and how we can use those experiences and emotions to return to a place of love.

Love is our default setting. Everything else has simply been programmed into our mind since birth.

We long to release the shackles of a fear-based existence, but it's become our comfort zone.

It's easier to stay in the pain, the hurt and the fear than it is to take a good hard look at who we truly are and to do the deep inner work to release the pain and move forward with love.

MY INVITATION TO YOU

Raising Wild Birds is an invitation for you to look inward: to reflect on the patterns in your life, reconnect to your inner child and learn to live from a place of pure, unconditional love. With this new sense of awakening and love that rises within you, you'll begin to radiate that out into the world – to friends, family, colleagues, online connections and beyond – to create a ripple effect that allows you to make the difference you've always desired.

You, beautiful soul, always knew you were destined for more, always knew you were just a little bit different and weren't going to be entirely fulfilled with a 'regular' life.

I see you.

I hear you.

I believe in you.

I trust you.

I love you.

This book will activate your own inner magic and wisdom, if you are willing to open, soften and allow it to take root in your heart.

At first you may want to read it through in order, taking the time to use the journal prompts for deeper reflection and self-growth. And at other times it will call you to turn directly to a certain page; maybe you'll notice the synchronicity in a number, an image, or words on the page.

Allow yourself to *feel* into these nudges; don't overthink them. Close your eyes and feel the sensations, notice the thoughts that spring into your mind, acknowledge your emotions and then let them go.

You have all the answers you'll ever need hidden deep within you.

This book will simply help you to make deeper connections with your inner wisdom; to feel supported, see the light that shines within you and hear the potent whispers from your soul.

I honour you for being here and doing this profound healing work that will not only help heal your own inner struggles and challenges but also will help to collectively heal others. Sharing the light and spreading the love is a beautiful way to live, but without looking inward at our own shadow side, our darkness, our grief, we can never truly step into our fullest, brightest and most brilliant potential.

There's so much more I could have written in this book: so many delicious life stories that played a part in reconnecting me to my empowered feminine, remembering the essence of who I am, what I came here to do and who I came here to be.

My wish is that this book may become, in part, your blueprint for life: something you can learn from, play with and use to empower your choices and raise your magical, unique and potent vibration.

LOVE

This is a book about love.

But not your typical clichéd romance with a Hollywood ending. So many 'love' stories aren't about love anyway – they're filled with infatuation, obsession, fear, pain, control, resentment, sadness or anger.

My love story is about pure, unconditional love and how we have to find that within ourselves and the world around us before we can truly love, or be loved, completely. It's about learning to recognise when we're acting from a place of fear instead of love, especially the kind of fear that masks itself as love. Illusions of love: making everything fit into a preconceived vision of love and ignoring the warning signs.

In sharing my words with you, I'm playing my part in ripping up those preconceived notions and ideas we've collectively been fed since the day we were born, and offering you an alternative way to live, breathe, thrive and succeed.

Throughout this book, I use the term 'The Universe' to describe the invisible energetic force that we can tap into to feel supported and whole. I believe that this energy source resides within each of us rather than being an invisible entity somewhere in the heavens. It's my own personal preference so please feel free to replace it with a word that resonates more deeply within your own soul – such as Source, Oneness or God.

A MESSAGE OF HOPE

Raising Wild Birds was conceived, nurtured and written across a period of huge change and shifts in human consciousness.

2020 saw a global pandemic which affected so much in our lives that we previously took for granted, and by 2021, things began to look very different. Huge protests against vaccine mandates took place across the world as many countries created systems that caused huge divides and separation in society. From the outside, as an empath, Starseed and lightworker, this was (and still is) incredibly hard to witness. As I returned to my writing in 2022 and 2023, so much deception and darkness was being brought into the light globally which, although difficult for many people to accept, will ultimately (I believe), push us all into a new and more connected and peaceful way of living.

I feel that at this point in time, humanity needs more messages of hope and love. Those who are now seeing the world with a new perspective need to know they're not alone; that others see them, hear them and can understand or empathise with how they're feeling and offer support, love and opportunity for transformation.

My hope is that this book will do that for you. I'm offering you my stories and experiences, encoded with love, channelled words and ancient wisdom, as a way to create small shifts in human consciousness; to throw my pebble into the sea and watch the ripples spread far and wide.

BREATHING THIS BOOK INTO LIFE

Until 2021, I'd spent almost a decade barely breathing: gentle, shallow, barely-there breaths; quiet, unassuming, and afraid of what might happen if I truly breathed in life, stepped out of my comfort zone and danced with the wild woman within.

It wasn't always like this of course. Once upon a time, I was a vibrant, young gym-obsessed personal trainer with a passion for weight training and getting hot, sweaty and out of breath. I loved rugged cliff path hikes or walks around the country lanes of my home island of Jersey, while any errand around town was always done at high speed with a desire to pack as much into my day as the air I breathed into my lungs.

So what changed?

2011 was a pivotal year, with the sad ending of a beautiful soulmate relationship, the heartbreaking loss of my beloved Persian cat and a return to being a single parent in an economy where the cost of living seemed to rise constantly. In the summer of 2012, I developed a health issue that took over 10 months to diagnose and in the meantime left me rushing to the bathroom multiple times a day. A short course of steroids helped a little but I intuitively felt this medication was shortening my life; like I'd never reach my dream of living to at least a hundred years young if I continued to take them. Various diet changes made little difference, but a return to vegetarianism and later a plant-based (vegan) diet definitely helped.

By 2013, financial issues came to a head and after having swapped my car for a cheaper-to-run model, and let go of all the little luxuries I'd known in my life since starting full-time work at nineteen, I finally gave in and swapped our lovely bungalow in the countryside for somewhere less expensive. To say I felt low is an understatement. The daily issues of bloating, diarrhoea and fatigue caused by an auto-immune bowel condition made me feel unfeminine, unhappy, and un-me.

Over the next few years, I drifted further and further away from the real Lorraine – the fizzy, social butterfly with the bright smile. I stayed indoors or by myself a lot, avoided meals out and exercised less and less. Of course, it wasn't all sadness and gloom, I have so many beautiful, happy memories of this decade which saw my daughters grow up from primary school children to amazing young adults. Plus there were holidays abroad, impromptu sunsets by the beach and the opportunity to teach my plant-based cooking at college, in the media and on local television. And if you know me personally or follow my social media, you'll know I'm an incredibly positive person, always smiling, always lifting others and spreading a little love and sunshine wherever I go.

So, how did I turn it all around and end up here, on my sparkly new laptop on the sofa, looking out on a plant-filled patio with the warm summer breeze blowing in, feeling supported, loved, vibrant, confident and ready to step up and share my story with the world?

And how did I learn to breathe again?

2013 was the year I started to show up regularly in my business on social media, and by 2015 I had found an incredible network of women who offered support, love and inspiration on a daily basis. Facebook was a completely different entity back then and so many gorgeous relationships and genuine connections were made – many of which I still value deeply today. While I'd always been interested in anything spiritual, holistic or rooted in self-growth, I delved much deeper into these areas from around this time. I remember reading *The Celestine Prophecy* (James Redfield), *Eat Pray Love* (Elizabeth Gilbert), *Get Rich Lucky B*tch* (Denise Duffield-Thomas) and so many other fantastic books that helped me to look inward, reflect on and understand my behaviour patterns and make transformative changes.

Having finished my Open University degree in 2015 (in English Literature and Creative Writing), I embarked on a period of investing as much time and energy as I could in learning everything about running a business in the online space. Because I still didn't have a great deal of financial security, investing my time in learning was the best and only solution for me.

Over the years I'd briefly been introduced to tarot cards but didn't really 'get it' – my logical brain always trying to figure it out, understand and make connections. But then I discovered a beautiful soul in Texas (through the power of the internet), with long flowing pink hair, butterfly tattoos and a magnetic energy that shouted *'I'm showing up as the best version of me and you must too!'* Brittney Carmichael was (is) her name and I followed her weekly 'Woo-Woo Wednesday' tarot card readings with enthusiasm, excitement and an open mind. Every week, the collective message felt like it was created just for me, and yet here were hundreds of other women feeling exactly the same way. The energy we felt watching Brit's live videos together was phenomenal and truly opened my mind and heart to a whole new world. When I treated myself to a pack of oracle cards a few months later, it became apparent very quickly that I share Brit's innate intuitive gifts. Over the years we've got to know each other more personally, discovering we're both Starseeds here to spread our love and light, as humans shift into this new era of heightened consciousness – the Age of Aquarius. I'm truly grateful to Brit for consistently showing up and shining her unique 'rainbow sparkle magic' with so much love and passion and for leading the way in feminine empowerment and teaching women how to tap into their soul's wisdom.

Another beautiful Starseed and lightworker soul to come into my world at around the same time was Rebecca Campbell, author of *Light is the New Black*, *Rise Sister Rise* and her latest gift to the world, *Letters to a Starseed*. The first time I heard Rebecca speak at a Hay House event in London in 2015, her energy blew me away. The group visualisation was so powerful that I still get chills when I think about it! Reading *Light Is the New Black* was the first book to introduce me to the term 'lightworker' and I resonated instantly with everything she wrote. It was like so many pieces of the puzzle suddenly came together for me. Understanding why I'd felt different at school, why I wasn't keen on getting drunk and partying every weekend, why a regular 9-5 job and traditional British lifestyle just didn't fit and why simplicity, honesty and integrity mattered so much more to me.

It's no surprise that within a few months of Rebecca and Brit appearing in my life, I pivoted literally overnight away from my twenty-plus year career as a freelance personal trainer, massage therapist and nutrition consultant, food coach and plant-based cooking teacher into intuitive copywriting – following my lifelong passion for words, language and communication. I've always known that I would write a book, but I never had any idea what it would be about. In my nutrition work, I wrote at least ten digital plant-based recipe books (e-books) and cooking guides, but still knew that there was an actual, real published book (or three!) in me somewhere.

As you'll find out later in this book, 2020 and 2021 were hugely pivotal years for me and included me finally taking the plunge and investing in the Unbound Writers Mastermind group course with Nicola Humber at the Unbound Press that ultimately led me to this point here today, writing this book and being published by a company that resonates so deeply with my heart. The *Unbound* way of writing, living and being.

While the book was originally going to be finished in 2020, and then 2021, ultimately it's taken until 2024! Not because the writing process was slow or difficult, but because the collective energy just wasn't right. With so much going on in the world and energy shifting on an almost weekly basis, it was as if I had an intuitive nudge that I needed to wait until after this crazy time.

Now, looking back, I know that the book I would have written in 2020, 2021 or 2022 (the 'lost' years) would have been drastically different from the one you're reading today. It feels right to me now and I hope it drops lovingly into your lap at the perfect moment after so much global turbulence and huge collective shifts.

THE ERA OF
BARELY BREATHING IS OVER

Being committed to walking every day for two years from February 2022 has shifted and propelled me into new levels and dimensions of growth, love and abundance. I'm excited to be finally embracing life more fully with huge lung-expanding deep breaths, allowing the energy of my life force to flow through me.

Before you turn the page and jump to the next chapter, I invite you to pause.

Place one hand on your heart and take a beautiful deep breath in through your nose, and a long slow breath out through your mouth.

And again.

And again.

Any time you feel stressed, anxious, overwhelmed or simply feel the need to reconnect to yourself, just do this one simple thing.

'Breathing is the essence of life, breathe deeply, live fully.'

– Gabriella Goddard

Journal Notes: Breathing

These notes from my journal offer an insight into my journalling process and how asking myself question after question leads to deeper and deeper insights from within. I believe that our soul always holds the answers we need, if only we pause to listen.

In my younger years, I simply knew this as a type of 'gut instinct'; a feeling that always meant that I made the right choices for me (even if they looked like the wrong choices from outside!).

I invite you in to my private journal space so that my thoughts, words and ideas may prompt you to reconnect with the threads of wisdom living within you.

I can't relax into breathing, why is that?

How can I crack open and feel?

Whatever is blocking me, I know I'll find through my breath.

I know as I work through these 'issues' and clear everything that the ability to breathe fully will come back but it may be the last thing. Perhaps one day I'll realise I'm breathing freely again.

Once the breath is clear, I'll have naturally shifted many of my energetic blocks.

In my visualisations, I need to visualise myself breathing freely.

This might even be why I'm not exercising much because I've become scared to fully breathe (= scared to fully live!).

Whatever is blocking my success and abundance can be cleared through breathing (i.e. just living!! Live fully = breathe fully).

Why do I find conscious breathing difficult? Perhaps exercise is a way to breathe again? Is this where mountains and hikes will come into play? I intuitively know they're going to play a huge part in my life.

Breathing is freedom and life

Breathing brings opportunities

Breathing clears blocks

**Swap out 'breathing' for 'living fully' in those sentences and they would still be 100% true...

Living fully is freedom and life

Living fully brings opportunities

Living fully clears blocks

So maybe there's my perfect two-pronged approach? Living fully AND doing breath work!

I started thinking earlier about doing a breath work class (or yoga with breathing) and I realised that I create obstacles straight away. It brings up feelings of 'I'm not good at that'. If I'm bad at something it's easier not to try. Uncomfortable flashback to being bad at the audible breaths in Bikram yoga classes!

Why was I so afraid of being heard when deep down I crave being seen and heard?

But what if I did try?

How might it feel?

(Just realised that I jump straight to being good at something and avoid ever visualising being in the discomfort.)

OK, so... sit in the discomfort.

Ask – when was another time I felt this way? What happened?

LIVE THE LIFE.

WRITE THE BOOK.

DO THE THINGS.

BREATHE.

I MEDITATED EVERY DAY FOR A YEAR

Throughout my entire adult life, meditation has always been sitting on the periphery. It's something I tried occasionally and while I was never consistent in any practice, I always held this inner knowing that meditation would be a key factor in my 'success' – whatever that looked like.

Like many people, I felt some kind of resistance to meditation. I couldn't put this into words, but made excuses about not having time (oh the irony!) or that it was just a bit 'too slow' for my preferred fast-paced way of life in my twenties and early thirties. I loved weight training, short bursts of cardio and cliff walks. I had young children and an active lifestyle. Sitting still for twenty minutes just wasn't going to happen!

And it wasn't just the physical blocks – my mind ran at 100mph. No, in fact, probably even faster than that! As a

Gemini sun with a mercurial mind (Gemini is ruled by quick-witted Mercury), my mind never stopped either. It wasn't an anxious mind, but simply a curious and creative one that loved learning and felt completely bored just watching TV!

Decades later, I still have that same witty, creative and curious mind, but regular, daily meditation (and other practices that I will share later in the book) has brought me a sense of calm stability, clarity and focus. I still think of multiple ideas every day, am still passionate about learning and frequently end up down internet rabbit holes researching something new, but it all has a more grounded energy.

Gone is the scatty, easily burnt-out energy of my youth. In its place is a serene, action-taking, gentle energy that fuels me closer and closer to my dreams and desires.

Perhaps part of that comes with age too. When we're running around after young children and being asked 'why?' a thousand times a day, life never seems to have many calm, serene moments. (Except when they're asleep!)

At some point, from around 2015 onwards, I decided to release the old story that I didn't have time for meditation and began to embrace it regularly – although not on a daily basis. I remember doing lots of gratitude-themed guided visualisations and meditations at this time of my life as I stepped into a higher version of me; moving into our (what was then) dream house, beginning a new part-time teaching role and later starting a home-education journey with my youngest daughter.

By 2019, I was using guided meditations far more regularly and when I broke my ankle in September that year, I added in 'bone healing' meditations – which I believe had a positive effect on my swift physical recovery.

During December 2020, after the craziness of a global pandemic and lockdown periods, I knew I was ready to shift more layers of the 'old' me and take another step towards my highest potential. I stepped into 2021 with a new energy, fuelled by my 'word of the year' – deliberate.

I wanted to be deliberate about every action, every day. If I chose to relax and watch Netflix with a huge bowl of pasta, I would do it deliberately, with love, knowing that this is what my body and mind wanted and needed in that moment. Every action in my business and on social media would be fuelled by that same essence of deliberate energy – doing everything on purpose, not just mindlessly scrolling or wasting time on something that didn't light me up.

In addition to these deliberate actions, I also made a pact to create space in all areas of my life: physically, emotionally, energetically, spiritually and financially. This included things like: decluttering areas of the home, donating clothes, letting go of old letters and cards, unsubscribing from email newsletters, deleting old computer files, creating a new spreadsheet for finances, removing myself from old Facebook groups and blocking whole days 'off' in my diary to allow for creativity, flow and ME-time.

(This is still an ongoing process. It's something that I recommit to every few months to clear space in my home, business, body and mind.)

My final pact to myself at the end of 2020 was to go into the new year meditating every day. And I'm very proud to say that I actually did it! Every single day of 2021. And since then, every single day of 2022 and 2023 and I'm still meditating every day in 2024. (I don't see myself ever stopping now!)

HOW MEDITATION CHANGED MY LIFE

Despite the epic challenges of the global pandemic during 2021, the ongoing fear-mongering by the media and general sense of uneasiness within the community, I felt a profound sense of calm. **Unshakeable. Grounded. Sovereign.**

This wasn't all due to meditation alone of course, but the meditation enhanced and deepened my connection to me; to my inner wisdom, my soul's whispers, my truth. Every day I grew more rooted in alignment to my truth.

Knowing that I had a meditation practice to return to each day gave me a sense of comfort, just like knowing you have a safe home, a warm bed and food in the fridge.

I found a routine that worked for me – using guided meditations before bed – and stuck with it. I try to meditate for around 15-30 minutes, depending on what time I go to bed. Sometimes I add in an extra one in the morning or mid-afternoon, always intuitively led. This practice has now become my baseline, my new normal. Nothing will stop me meditating every day!

Many schools of thought say that it's not proper meditation if you're lying down, but I haven't quite yet managed to sit still, upright with legs crossed without fidgeting! When I fidget I get distracted and lose the flow, so lying down is currently my preferred go-to method.

Hint: Don't wait until conditions are perfect before starting daily meditation. Just do it today – even for five minutes. Then repeat tomorrow. And the next day. If you miss a day, don't stress about it. Just get straight back into it the next day. As they say, 'Done is better than perfect'!

NAVIGATING THE WORLD AS A LIGHTWORKER AND STARSEED

Navigating the world as a lightworker, Starseed or empath comes with its own set of unique challenges. We may have grown up believing our sensitive nature, kindness and compassion were faults or a weakness and that we had to be 'stronger', or learn to toughen up to survive in this world.

The more I learned about being a lightworker and Starseed, the more I understood that my presence here is enough. Simply showing up as me, in my authentic truth, can make a difference, spark a transformative thought or kickstart a collective tsunami.

As I realised this, it became easier and easier to be gentle with myself; to let go of the self-imposed chains I'd wrapped around myself in the form of perfectionism and needing to fit in.

And in being more gentle and kind with myself, my boundaries, self-care and self-love all improved. It became a positive, upward-spinning cycle of joy and fulfilment.

I realised that life can look totally different to the expectations we've held for so long and that ultimately, if we want something to change, then we have to start by looking inward.

Perhaps that's why you're here…

To get curious. To ask deeper questions.

To take care of your own healing, growth and happiness.

To just simply BE.

And then, ultimately, to step into your power, shine your light and create a ripple effect of transformation around the world.

Perhaps, like me, you see yourself as a visionary, a catalyst, a leader and role model, shaping the way for others to follow.

Being a leader doesn't mean you have to be shouting about your gifts, talents and ideas from the rooftops. It's not a leader in the masculine, patriarchal, corporate manager sense. When you're a lightworker you're here to radiate light, love and positivity in a gentle way that guides others to become the best version of themselves.

Of course, being a lightworker doesn't mean that your life is filled with light and nothing else! In fact, it means often having to wade through the sticky black darkness within your mind and body before being transformed and finding a new level of purpose, connectedness and passion. But if you resonate with being a lightworker, you're well equipped to handle the journey, I promise. It may seem difficult at times, but you have everything you need to not only overcome all your personal challenges but also to continuously evolve and transform.

Sometimes, in your work as a lightworker, or in your personal relationships, you'll trigger people. Their reaction is not a reflection of you, but of their own inner pain, misalignment and energy blocks. It can be tough, particularly with those closest to you, but ultimately you're here to shine brighter and to lift others along the way.

Know that you've incarnated here, at this point in time, for a very important reason.

It's time to grab your journal…

(I find that writing by hand, on paper, slows down my mind and allows space for channelled thoughts, ancient wisdom or deeply held patterns to come to the surface. Sometimes slowly forming into a bigger picture, other times appearing all at once, faster than I can write them down!)

Journal Prompts:

- How have you felt different to others over your lifetime?

- What comes so naturally to you that it doesn't feel difficult or like 'work' at all?

- What do you know about being a lightworker and Starseed?

If these are new terms to you, take some time to research lightworkers and Starseeds further over the coming days. The connections you make – whether in your mind or in real life physical connections with other like-minded souls – always happen for a reason.

GRATITUDE JOURNALLING
AND FORGIVENESS

There are many different ways to journal. Some love to write daily, like a diary entry. Some love to use their notebook as a witness to their deepest thoughts and fears. Some love to use the practice of intimate writing to connect with their inner voice or guardian angels to receive guidance and reassurance.

There are no right or wrong ways to journal.

Over a decade ago, I read a brilliant book called *The Gratitude Diaries* by Janice Kaplan. It was warm, friendly and extremely funny, and it was the catalyst for me starting a 'gratitude journal'. Every evening before bed I'd write down ten things I was grateful for that day. Initially, I remember writing things like 'a warm house, hot water, a cosy bed' and so on. But before long I began to see a shift. Suddenly I was writing about 'the huge bumble bee on the pink rose in the garden', or the warm, fuzzy sensation I had from hugging my daughter when she was upset.

This daily gratitude practice became a non-negotiable part of my life as it brought me so much inner peace, calmness and connection to nature. It really was the beginning of a long period of huge transformation and personal growth – some of which I'm sharing in this book.

Alongside my experiences of gratitude journalling, I soon came across a beautiful Hawaiian Ho'oponopono prayer for forgiveness:

I'm sorry. Please forgive me. Thank you. I love you.

This can be used as part of a forgiveness practice to let go of old blocks and energy that we're holding onto about people that have hurt us, or our own actions that we're not proud of.

For example, being angry at yourself for staying in a toxic relationship for too long, or for spending too much money and getting into debt.

I began to use this forgiveness practice in my longer journalling sessions, particularly around the full moon – a time to release all the things that are no longer serving us. Again, it was a truly important step for me in my personal growth journey.

Some other books I read around that time that you might enjoy are:

- *The Celestine Prophecy* by James Redfield
- *The Cosmic Ordering Service* by Barbel Mohr
- *Psychology of the Hero Soul* by Sharif N. Khan
- *The Road Less Travelled* by M. Scott Peck

RAISING WILD BIRDS – A METAPHOR FOR LEARNING TO LIVE FROM A PLACE OF LOVE, NOT FEAR

In this book, I'm about to share with you stories, insights and ideas that encompass my personal journey and experiences through life, through the lens of reflection as a woman who now possesses the awareness to recognise when she's falling into old patterns or behaviours of fear-based thinking, being or doing.

I now know how important it is to be gentle and non-judgemental with ourselves as we go through periods of deep self-reflection, because 'younger me' didn't know any different. We didn't yet have the awareness, knowledge or abilities to make better choices. And ultimately, we need to go through these periods of challenges and failure in order to grow and become exactly who we're meant to be, at the perfect time.

And it's the same with our parents and grandparents. We may feel a certain way about aspects of how they raised us, but they were only doing the best they could in that moment. Part of our healing journey will always include gratitude, forgiveness and love for all the people in our lives, as that is the only way to move on and truly shift our habits, patterns and beliefs and live the peaceful, fulfilled life we've always dreamed of.

To reflect this lifelong journey of learning, awareness, growth and understanding, I've divided *Raising Wild Birds* into three parts:

Part One: The Baby Bird

In Part One, the core theme is based around being stuck in a fear mindset and how that can be seen in our everyday words, thoughts and actions. When we're stuck in a place of fear, we are often afraid of being truly seen and carry a sense of longing, as well as unhealthy attachments to people, places and objects. We usually feel rejection deeply which causes us pain which we project onto others, cause unnecessary arguments and stress in our lives, or carry the pain internally which may resurface in patterns of self-sabotage. In our early childhood, we might have felt different to others, so we developed patterns of staying quiet or conforming to fit in, which has the later effect of struggling to be heard and feeling like we don't have a voice.

Part Two: Learning to Fly

In Part Two, the core themes are developing awareness, embracing vulnerability and stepping into the unknown. It's about realising there's no point waiting to be 'saved', and that you are able to release attachment, soften your heart and give new things a try. It's about embracing failure and trying again and again until new patterns are fully integrated and embodied. As you move into new stages of life, you will learn how to better understand and handle rejection, increase your capacity to receive love and lighten your energetic load. You're more likely to call in support, share a little more of who you are behind the mask and push through new cycles of awareness and growth.

Part Three: Soaring High

In Part Three, the core themes are based around empowerment and embodiment; finally becoming your true self and sharing who you really are with the world with confidence, presence and love. At this stage, you're making consistent progress in showing up, speaking up and creating your own version of a desire-led life. You have created a supportive network of friends, colleagues and connections who guide and empower you to step into your potential and shine brilliantly. You are devoted to your own personal growth and physical, emotional and spiritual wellbeing and have discipline in your day-to-day activities which leads to further progress and possibilities. As you soar high through life, you feel an inner harmony of empowered masculine and feminine energies, experience sensuality and pleasure frequently and live a life filled with gratitude and expansion. You've planted seeds and are reaping the rewards, taking quantum leaps at certain times that propel you forward into new situations that you never once imagined were possible.

PART ONE

THE BABY BIRD

FEELING DIFFERENT

For so much of my life, I felt out of place. I wondered why people couldn't see things the same way I did and why the world was so cruel.

As a child in the early 1980s, I vividly remember all the news reports about animal cruelty in the cosmetics industry and watching as activist groups released hundreds of white rabbits, dogs and other animals from testing laboratories. Watching Greenpeace and anti-whaling protesters in the oceans trying to stop the mass slaughter of these incredible creatures left me sad and confused. Why did people want to kill, hurt or mistreat animals and why did I feel so scared to voice my opinion and powerless to help? I knew in my heart that they were doing something important, right and powerful in their mission but the good girl in me couldn't imagine putting myself in the firing line, risking being hurt by riot police, arrested or worse.

I lived with the guilt of being too scared to step away from that 'good girl' persona for many years and only more recently realised that being the activist in this sense isn't in my soul contract. I'm here to create change in other ways – like writing this book and sharing valuable content online through the power of words, or teaching people the infinite benefits of plant-based cooking for their health, the animals and the environment. We can all help and support the causes and issues we're passionate about in our own unique ways. We don't all have to march down the streets with placards; plenty can be done quietly and powerfully behind the scenes too. If you're living with feelings of guilt or feeling like you 'should' be doing more, I invite you to take some time to reflect more deeply within and to journal on your feelings and experiences before letting them go. *(Writing on paper and burning your words on a full moon is a powerful time to release this negative energy.)*

Looking back, I realise how being tapped into my natural intuition from a young age has helped me to find my own way in life to offer this guidance and support. As a lightworker, I'm here to make a difference by spreading love and being an inspiration: a role model, a teacher, a guiding light. We're all here for different reasons and some of us can inspire, empower and activate change more gently, softly, subtly. Our presence is enough.

At fifteen, I became a vegetarian. *(It's much easier for children to start younger these days as there's so much information available to support and inspire both them and their parents. So if you have a young child who has already made the animal-meat connection and wants to change their diet, there is so much help available for you. I promise it does not have to be stressful, expensive or difficult!)* I remember being so happy when, as a teenager, the UK beauty retailer The Body Shop opened in our town as it sold only cruelty-free products and was a pioneer in changing the way we think about testing products on animals and in fair trade for farmers and producers abroad.

In my early twenties, I took a new career path and trained in fitness, massage and nutrition so that I could use my new skills, passion and own experiences around food (I'd suffered with IBS from the age of thirteen) to support and teach others. I remember my parents being concerned that this wasn't a 'proper career' and worried that I was making a wrong decision, but even through years of financial insecurity as a freelancer, I stayed true to my heart, my soul and my inner desire to help others transform their lives and achieve the happiness they desire.

My natural gifts of intuition and energy healing were incredibly beneficial to me as a massage therapist. Without realising it, these innate skills were transmuted through the power of touch during massage treatments to channel ancient healing wisdom for my clients. I sensed, felt and simply 'knew' things about each person's body and many of my clients felt a profound sense of relaxation and transformation after a treatment. In hindsight, this is probably why I also found it so tiring because I was absorbing so much of their negative 'pain' energy and didn't know how to fully protect myself energetically.

As an adult, I struggled with feeling out of place for many years before finally realising and accepting that my differences were what made me unique and that my passion and purpose were what drove me to stay committed to my beliefs. Working in health and fitness naturally led me down the path of healthy eating, which wasn't embraced to the same extent (or at all!) by family and friends who were happy to stick to a regular British diet and lifestyle. It was hard for me to understand that many people could never even contemplate that there were other diet and lifestyle options that could bring better health, more energy, more vibrancy and more connection to planet Earth.

There was a period in time where I felt like my way was 'the right way' and therefore was guilty of judging others for the choices they made. But part of *my* journey has been about learning to let go of those judgements and to focus on my own path and release any attachments to other people's actions. There's a beautiful sense of inner freedom that comes with this release that really has to be experienced.

When it came to alcohol, I'm still not entirely sure which came first: becoming more 'awakened' and tapped into my intuition and not wanting to numb those sensations with alcohol, or giving up alcohol and having more time and clarity to create space for the awakening to unfold…

Either way, *not* drinking alcohol meant that I saw the world differently.

In our modern Western culture, refusing an alcoholic drink is an act of defiance! It goes so strongly against British culture that at first you have to be armed with a steady stream of excuses to ensure you stay sober *and* still fit in!

Ultimately, part of the issue is this innate desire to fit in; to be part of a tribe, a community, a group. In ancient times, being alone and shunned from the village would have meant certain death. This need is hardwired into our DNA which makes stepping outside of the norm not only difficult personally, but will also gift you a steady stream of commentators who will be happy to share all the reasons why your way is wrong!

Ultimately, whether it's animal products, alcohol, experimental vaccines or something else, saying no to things that other people readily accept as the only way to live a normal life will push you to your edges, giving you ample opportunities to fail, fall in line or become part of an argument or a statistic. Globally, we've seen so much anger, sadness and division caused during the Covid pandemic as different countries chose different ways to manage and control the situation. Can you imagine the push-back and protests that would have happened if

Governments tried to force everyone to become vegan, give up alcohol or stop smoking?!

Standing Up for What You Believe In

You can stand up for your beliefs and live your truth in a way that is loud and visible and actively try to bring others on the journey with you. Or you can do it quietly and just for yourself; staying aligned to your truth and living a life that feels authentic for you.

For me, the constant thread throughout my lifelong journey has been about cooking food from scratch every day using an abundance of fresh vegetables and enjoying food at the table with my children. It didn't matter whether I was vegetarian, an omnivore or plant-based, everything we ate was connected to nature, made with love and enjoyed as a family.

My mum cooked every day when I was a child, and while some of my childhood in the 1980s did veer towards the new labour-saving trend of convenience food, I was lucky enough to grow up knowing how 'real food' tasted, how it was grown (my dad loved growing vegetables and fruit) and how to cook meals from scratch on a budget with as little waste as possible.

Standing up for what you believe in is the same energy vibration as living a life in alignment with your truth, your core values. When you live a life this way, you begin to feel more centred and calm, more joyful and effortlessly able to attract in more of what you love.

Just like compound interest, your health and happiness will grow exponentially over time the more regular 'deposits' you make – i.e. the more good stuff you do for your body, mind and soul every day.

Journal Prompts:

- What do you believe in? What's really important to you?

- How do you feel when someone else has opposite views or an entirely different lifestyle?

- Do you feel that your way is the 'right way'? Dive deeper into why you might feel the need to be right, or what it is about the 'wrong way' that creates so much negative energy, anger or rage inside you.

- What are your core values?

- Are they really your values? Or are they your society's values, your parents' values or your partner's values?

- How would it feel to continue living life in a way that isn't aligned to your values, to your core truth? What physical or mental health issues have you developed because of this misalignment?

- How would it feel to step beyond your comfort zone and beyond the regular way of life in your country or culture to follow your own path?

LOSING MY VOICE

'You're tone deaf!', my classmate Sally shouted in my ear when I was just five or six years old. Hurt, embarrassed and feeling a deep sense of shame at being different from most of the little girls in my class with their angelic voices, this kick-started a pattern of hiding my voice that was to carry on well into my forties.

Whenever a woman could sing really well – whether that was professionally or at a karaoke bar – I felt a deep sense of jealousy. When my teenage boyfriend fancied Wendy James (Transvision Vamp) and Blondie, I felt a rage deep inside my gut. But with no tools to know how to deal with these feelings, inevitably my insecurity and anger popped up in other ways: sarcasm, snide comments, picking fights, numbing with food or alcohol or running away from situations.

I was so afraid that my lack of singing ability would be highlighted and I'd be made to look stupid in public, that I avoided any kind of karaoke bar situation. On the odd occasion I was ever tipsy enough to get on stage with a big group of friends, I'd make sure I was at the back, a long way away from the microphone!

As a young girl in the Brownies and Girl Guides, I often had to go to church for Sunday services. Still gripped by the fear of being 'outed' for my inability to sing in tune, I mimed to the hymns, but always scared I'd be caught and told off! (I wasn't! Phew!)

During childhood, I suffered with tonsillitis a lot, to the point where I had my tonsils removed at seven years old. I still remember the experience vividly. The pain was excruciating but the nurses wouldn't let us eat ice cream until we'd finished the scratchy burnt toast! Perhaps they thought it would help us heal faster, but I just thought they were being mean! *(Which in hindsight was probably the start of my distrust of authority and the medical system.)*

Nowadays, doctors are more reluctant to remove tonsils as they're actually an important gland and part of the immune system. For me, not only was it part of a lifetime of 'throat issues', but it also meant that every time I had a cold or a virus, it went to my chest and gave me a horrible cough. Even now, the fear that overtakes my body when I feel I'm about to launch into an uncontrollable coughing fit in public is enough to make me hide away at home for a week or two until I've fully recovered!

Clearly, I came into this world with a need to heal my throat chakra and learn to speak my truth and use my voice.

While there were many areas of life where I was always too afraid to speak up – like in relationships or friendships – choosing instead to 'people please' and just be the good girl, I found my avenue for speaking my truth was through health and nutrition.

All I needed to do was live in a way that felt right to me, choosing a life aligned to my values and share that experience with others.

Journal Prompts:

- Do you suffer with throat conditions frequently? Were you always sick with tonsillitis as a child?

- Do you have a lot of coughing fits or lose your voice after a virus? How do these illnesses make you feel? What fear, anxiety, stress or anger rises within you?

- Energetically, what do you feel your throat conditions are connected with?

- Was there a physical trauma in your childhood connected with your throat? Or around not being able to speak up? Take some time to reflect and journal on this.

- At some point in your life, did you have to keep quiet about something? Were you forced into secrecy? Were your parents always telling you to be quiet? Did you have a sibling who took up a lot of your parents' time or who dominated the energy in the room?

Important note: *I'm not a licensed coach or a therapist. If you feel like these prompts might take you back into areas of your life you'd rather not revisit, or which might be incredibly painful, please seek the support of a qualified therapist who can guide you safely on a healing journey.*

Further research: *Find out more about the throat chakra online, on social media or in books. Learn how you can use specific techniques to heal and strengthen this area.*

THE COLOUR OF LOVE

We can't colour other people's lives for them. They have to be free to choose their own vivid technicolour world.

My mum loves purple. I hate purple.

I love yellow. My mum hates yellow.

When I was a child I had a lilac and purple bedroom. I don't remember ever choosing to have a purple room. But it was the 1970s and hence the colour du jour. My godmother, also named Lorraine, a beautiful, glamorous woman with long blonde hair and the tiniest waist, had a very elegant purple bedroom. Two-year-old me thought so anyway! The curtains were really long and draped on the floor, while the polyester bedspread was quilted and hung over the sides in pleats of sheer purple luxury. I often slept in that bed while my parents and godparents enjoyed dinner together and developed an affection for its softness that lulled me into dreamland.

The colour purple came up for discussion in a social media conversation in 2022 with Tara Jackson, an author, artist, Colour Mirrors expert and founder of Empathpreneurs® and Business Chakras® Alchemy. Many people expressed how much they loved purple and how it felt like a connection to higher realms and intuition. My reaction was the opposite to everyone else. While I'm deeply connected to my own intuition and my heart and crown chakras, I feel a strong dislike of the colour purple in almost anything manmade and synthetic! It's hard to put into words exactly *why* I feel this way.

When you suddenly get an intense feeling, especially a negative one, it's *always* worth exploring where that comes from and why you feel that way. Think of these reactions as a nudge from the Universe to look inward for answers.

I spent some time exploring all the different areas that came to mind: fashion and interiors, my made-up stories around the types of people who wear purple, my childhood, my relationship with my mother growing up and anything else that sprang to mind – like the image of my godmother's bedroom decor.

Growing up, your relationship with your mother goes through different phases. As a young child, you probably idolise her, want to copy her fashion style, and you spend much of your time with her. As you grow into your teens, the opposite often happens. Suddenly everything she does, wears or says is 'old fashioned and frumpy' and in complete contrast to how you feel as you blossom into a young woman with your own thoughts, ideas, passions and goals. In our teens, we're often embarrassed by our parents. We don't want to be seen in public with them in case they ruin our 'street cred', especially if the boy we fancy sees us all out in public together. *(Yes, I am thinking of a specific occasion walking with my parents in their matching 80s anoraks!)*

At some point, possibly when you have your own children, you might be drawn back together as you begin to understand the challenges she went through when you were young. For other mothers and daughters, the closeness comes far later in life, when their mother becomes a grandmother or reaches her seventies and eighties. And for others, the closeness is there throughout every stage of life while some never experience that true loving closeness, trust, honesty and mutual respect.

After sharing some of my thoughts and memories around the colour purple with Tara, she mentioned that yellow is its opposite colour. Instantly, I felt that deep belly warmth and fizz that you get when you suddenly see a connection.

Yellow makes me feel alive!

When I finished creating an online course in February 2022, I was drawn to a yellow jumper in my cupboard to take photos to promote it! The yellow felt like success, joy, happiness, spring, creativity. I had a gorgeous spaghetti-strapped, floaty yellow top I used to wear out to pubs and clubs fifteen years ago – which is still in my wardrobe as I can't bear to get rid of it!

Yellow represents sunshine, brightness, bouncy fun and happy memories to me.

Ironically, my mum *hates* yellow! Especially bright yellow, mustard and gold. I always remember her emphatically stating how much she hated both yellow and red! Even now, when I browse internet florist websites to buy flowers for her birthday, seeing bouquets with red and yellow flowers bring back negative childhood emotions, thoughts and feelings. Perhaps in sharing this story and releasing the attachment I hold in my body, I'll gradually heal those negative associations, layer by layer, and move forward without experiencing those strong thoughts and feelings every time.

This personal investigation into colour got me thinking about how it connects to this book's theme of love and fear. As a parent, choosing what your child wears or what colour to paint their room is colouring their life for them instead of letting them choose their own path. It's a way in which we project our own experiences of life and personal likes or desires onto others. With our own children, we effectively try to mould them into the child we expect them to be without ever stopping to listen to who they really are and how they wish to express themselves.

Of course, times are changing. This is 2022 planet Earth, not the 1920s or 1960s. But judgements, labels and prejudice still run riot across the world. Our perspective is entirely coloured by our own life experience. Our child-hood, our interactions with others, our culture, the country we live in, the job we do, our education level and even the amount of money we have in the bank – all play a tiny part in our perception of, and reaction to, every situation, every conversation, every relationship.

More and more people are realising that the key to healing major issues around the world starts with healing our own personal issues within. Even if we've had a beautiful childhood, with a secure family home and loving parents, we can still carry attachments and limiting beliefs to the experiences we've had.

You don't have to have been through severe trauma or pain, grief or illness to begin working on your inner self.

Any time you feel prompted to understand why you have a strong reaction to something or someone, that's your intuition whispering to you, nudging you to look within for the answers.

And it could be something as simple as a negative reaction to an Instagram post about the colour purple that kick-starts this whole process!

Journal Prompts:

- What strong feelings do you have around colour?

- Is there a specific colour you love or hate?

- If any strong emotions or physical sensations come up, that's a great place to start this self-reflection. Where do you feel it in your body? How does it feel?

- Where have you felt that before?

- What might it be connected to?

LOVE AND REJECTION

'If you love somebody let them go, for if they return,
they were always yours. And if they don't, they never were.'

– Kahlil Gibran

I first heard a similar version of this quote when I was about thirteen or fourteen years old and it stuck in my head, colouring my experiences of romantic love for many years. What I realise now, as a woman fast approaching fifty, is that I've carried a deep abandonment wound since birth (or maybe from past lives) that meant my reaction to certain experiences was one of rejection. And it wasn't pretty!

Every time a man left me, acted in a way I didn't understand or simply wasn't in the mood for sex, I felt a deeply painful sense of rejection. It made me make *every* situation about me.

If a partner didn't want sex, I believed he didn't love me or fancy me and that therefore I wasn't good enough and needed fixing in some way. In those reactive moments, I might have felt too fat, not sexy enough, or that he was interested in someone else! My mind ran off at 200mph and created whole scenarios about what was going on in this man's head – when in reality, he might just have been preoccupied, tired or just didn't feel like making love that night!

Sometimes, this reactive wound meant that I made bad decisions from a place of deep pain and lack. If you've ever got in touch with an old flame or flirted with the idea of someone new when your current relationship wasn't fulfilling your basic needs, then you'll understand the reactive energy I'm referring to here.

What I understand now, is that every time I sought a lightness, excitement or escape after those feelings of rejection burnt a hole in my gut, I was in fact running from myself and my own darkness. I needed to learn how to pause in those moments of rejection and look inward at the darkness, the grief and the pain, and not find solace in a person, food or a Bacardi-fuelled night out.

I'll be honest with you, it took me a long time to really get to grips with this, but that's just my personal journey, and yours will look entirely different.

In hindsight, I don't think I ever properly grieved the loss of my father in 2004. His cancer returned more aggressively just as my youngest daughter was born in the summer of 2003. And when I look back, I realise that over the next ten years I went through a lot of emotional turmoil that I never truly processed. My marriage ended (amicably), a four-year relationship with a true soulmate came to an abrupt end (at which point that abandonment wound was deeply triggered), I lost my beloved cat to cancer after thirteen years of pure unconditional love, plus the financial issues that led us to move out of our family home, swap my car for a cheaper model and finally, support my daughter through spinal surgery.

So, with the benefit of hindsight, I can now see how my thirties were filled with loss, grief and change that I never truly dealt with. I believe it's why I went on to develop an auto-immune gut condition and chronic fatigue which dominated my life for many years. The combination of all these factors led me to isolate myself more and more (despite being very active in the online business space), shy away from dating and remain single for most of my forties.

There was a part of me that believed that maybe I'd had my share of wonderful relationships and amazing intimacy and that perhaps I was destined to be single; the stereotypical 'single cat lady' (except with cute fluffy house bunnies too!).

As I became more and more aware of my own inner stories, I also connected in with the energy of my female ancestors. My mum, having lost her husband (my dad) when she was only sixty-two, has spent the last two decades alone (romantically), and my maternal grand-mother spent many years alone after divorce as a young mum and later when she was widowed in her seventies, while my paternal grandmother also outlived her husband by around 30 years.

For a while, I believed the 'story' that maybe it was just our family pattern to be strong, single females who didn't *need* a man. But that's not really true. While I can't speak for all my female relatives and ancestors, I know that I deeply crave the companionship, love, physical touch and intimacy of a soulmate partner. I may be perfectly happy in my everyday life as a single woman, but there's a huge part of me that isn't able to express itself fully and shine and its brightest light.

I also deeply feel that I'm here on planet Earth at this era in time to act as a **pattern interrupt**. Just because certain things have happened in my family before me doesn't mean they have to continue on into future generations.

When we make a decision to heal aspects of our lives, we not only change the future for our children and grandchil-dren, but we also heal the past, allowing our ancestors to sleep more peacefully among the stars.

Journal Prompts:

- How have your early experiences of love and romance coloured your expectations and shaped your life?

- Do you feel rejection deeply in your heart and soul? So deeply that it derails your emotions, your happiness and your life?

- How has rejection or grief shown up in your life? Have you been pushing these emotions down without dealing with them?

- Have suppressed emotions manifested as sickness, illness, disease or other health issues? Or as financial issues? Or as relationship issues?

- What parts of your rejection or grief story do you now understand or see differently?

- Write a letter to your younger self to let them know it's OK that they felt and acted that way, and that you forgive them for not knowing better.

Please note: I'm not a trained counsellor or therapist, so if these areas of personal reflection feel too deep and emotional for you to carry alone, please reach out to a qualified therapist for support as you navigate this part of your life

'Caged birds sing of freedom, free birds fly.'

— THOROLF RAFTO

AFRAID OF BEING SEEN

Notes from My Journal:

What does staying in the struggle bring me?

Why is it so comfortable in the discomfort?

In my life, I've noticed the paradox of staying stuck in the struggle and playing small while holding the desire to desperately want to be seen and heard.

What does playing small, staying in the darkness bring me?

Safety, in terms of not being seen – so just like in ancient human times, if I don't go outside then a predator can't get me!

What's scary about being out in the limelight, being successful?

I'm scared of it bringing me long work hours that my body or relationships can't cope with, more stress, having to outsource, building a team – I don't know if I want all that. But what if I had an amazing best-selling book (if you're reading this that may have actually come true!) and a team doing my social media, PR and marketing? That would be great right? Having a cleaner to support me felt good in the past. Going for facials and massage and investing in coaching is great, so why not building a team? I guess I'm worrying about something in the future so let's just leave that for now. It doesn't need to take up space in my head...

Why is it comfortable in the struggle?

It's an identity I've taken on. It's 'who I am' – except it's not!! What if I created a whole new reality? What if I created a whole new life that didn't involve struggle? How might that feel? Sure, there would be challenges, there always are in human life and the healing journey, but what if I chose another mindset, paid for a service or worked through more triggers?

I'm leaving behind the 'struggling single parent' identity and I'm going to become the woman I was always destined to be.

I want to be truly seen.

Showing up from victim mode never helped me to be seen. I just need to live my best life every moment of every day.

I need to let go of the excuses I have for why other women are successful and why it isn't possible for me.

If I simply live my life on my terms, then I will be seen. This is where I have to have FAITH. To surrender to the universe, (deep breath as I wrote that); to trust that everything will pan out as it's meant to if I follow my heart.

I want to be truly seen. We have to remember that relationships of all kinds aren't a competition. We're all in this together and are meant to rise and shine brighter, radiating light around the world and raising human consciousness.

DANCING WITH FEAR

Growing up as a white Western woman, Hollywood's classic rom-com movies led me to believe that the most desirable women looked and acted a certain way. One characteristic I picked up on was that the better a woman could dance, and the longer, more toned and shapely her legs, the more sexually attractive she was to men.

Compared to these women, I never felt good enough. While it didn't stop me dancing in nightclubs as a teenager and young woman, I did carry a belief that I was in some way inadequate because I couldn't properly dance.

This fuelled my personal theme of rejection because the story I concocted was: I can't dance like that and I don't look like that, so therefore I'm not attractive and it's the reason why I always feel rejected. And it wasn't just in the movie world that this story sprung up. Growing up in the 80s and early 90s, I was 'led' to believe that women who were successful in business had long slender legs and brunette hair – the polar opposite to me at 5 ft 4 with gorgeous girl-next-door curves and thick blonde hair.

When we stop to reflect on our behaviour – especially when we pour our thoughts onto paper – we can see how crazy our beliefs really are!

As I grew into a more confident woman and experienced beautiful relationships and became a mother, those thoughts disappeared most of the time. But any time dancing came up – like at a wedding or an event in daylight – I froze.

Every memory, story and image that was scorched into my mind came flooding back. I usually made excuses to stay at the table with a drink or excused myself to the bathroom – especially if it was a song with a rhythm that didn't feel natural to me. (*I've always loved pop and dance music though and would happily dance around at home with my daughters.*)

It's no surprise that dance involves a lot of letting go – and I knew that my body was too tense to let go. I was self-conscious and worried what people would think about me, never letting myself go and truly joining in the fun. I'd watch women who could dance like crazy, completely not bothered by how they looked or how others might perceive them. In hindsight, I always wore a mask in these situations, pretending I was having fun when often I just wanted to get out of there as fast as I could!

What if I just allowed myself to dance?

I signed up for a Latin American evening class back in 2006, shortly after my husband and I decided to split up. It felt like perfect timing – to do something that helped me to flow, be more feminine and, well it just felt right! Unfortunately, the class was almost entirely women which meant my female partner and I had to keep taking turns to dance the male and female parts – far too much for my brain to handle! I let my fear get in the way and stopped going after a couple of classes, making out that time and parental responsibilities were stopping me.

Letting a Man Lead the Way

I realise now, after much inner work, journalling and reflection on my limiting beliefs, that I've never truly allowed a man to lead me – in dance or in life. There was one moment at a house party back in the early 1990s when a young French guy told me to maintain eye contact as he tried to twirl me around in a 'swing' style. I felt deeply uncomfortable despite having a very easy friendship with this man. Eye contact is something that's so easy with certain people in certain situations, and yet at other times, we can be so afraid to lock eyes and open the windows to our own soul.

I know that I'm now ready to meet my King; a man who can lead me in life *and* on the dance floor. A man with whom I feel safe, secure and who soothes my nervous system.

Journal Prompts:

If any of my words and experiences have resonated with you today, I invite you to dig a little deeper to uncover more of the trapped energy and blocks beneath your feelings.

- When it comes to dancing, performing or speaking in public, what am I afraid of?

- Why am I afraid to be seen a certain way? Why do I even care about what others think?

- Am I afraid of sinking into my feminine and allowing a man to lead me?

LONGING FOR HOME

When I was twenty-one, I felt that something was missing. It was an intuitive feeling of longing that I couldn't entirely pinpoint or label, but I knew something big had to shift.

In my heart, I knew I had to leave my amazing boyfriend, our home, our cats and the life we'd started building together, and move back in with my parents.

There was no tangible event or negative experience to use as a reason for this massive shift, which meant that those close to me couldn't easily understand why I was seemingly throwing away a great relationship and a stereotypical 'happy' future.

(In my forties, I learned that Starseeds often have this 'longing' for home without any idea where 'home' actually is. This usually precedes a huge period of growth and transformation that changes your perspective forever.)

In those next couple of years, I focused mainly on my own health, fitness and wellbeing, which paved the way for the next door that opened, bringing with it a huge opportunity.

After being made redundant, and gifted over £1000 in redundancy pay, I embarked on a new career in nutrition and fitness, which in turn led to new connections, new friends and a whole host of new experiences that together formed a huge part of who I am today and the 'grown up' I've become.

That's the thing, of course. When one door closes, another opens. However difficult it feels shutting one door, it's an essential part of the growth process.

My new lifestyle and career in fitness led me to the sunny island of Jersey. A place where I would meet my future husband and father of my amazing daughters; a place where I would make many spiritual connections and deep friendships and a place I could call home.

Over the last couple of decades, I've experienced many more doors opening and new beginnings, and plenty of failures, endings and doors closing – not all of my own choice.

Through this bumpy journey of human life, I've been gifted the chance to develop my resilience, learn the true meaning of unconditional love and test my faith in the Universe.

When things are looking a little wonky in your life, lean into your intuition. Use meditation to tap into your inner wisdom and trust that everything will always be working out for you, even if it doesn't appear that way on the surface.

FEELING INVISIBLE

When it comes to love, life and business, we could all do with a strong dose of a visibility drug to give us the strength to stand up for what we believe in, to share our truth, to shout it from the rooftops when we're in love and to tell people how amazing they are so they too can shine a little bit brighter.

In one short romantic relationship a few years back, the theme of invisibility reared its ugly head, triggering emotions and self-sabotaging behaviours I thought I'd left behind in my thirties! In essence, I felt invisible through-out the whole of this short relationship because this man's words did not match his actions. It felt to me as if I didn't even exist, which – for someone so sunny, radiant and here to light up the world – was like hell!

To me, feeling invisible was like being trapped inside a birdwatching hide: I could see out but no one could see me or hear me and no one even knew I existed!

At the time, I wrote these words in my journal:

> **What's the scariest thing about feeling invisible?**
>
> For a Starseed here to light up the world, it feels like being put in a dark room and locked away.
>
> If you're invisible, no one gets to see your light.
>
> You can't fulfil the mission you came here to do.
>
> You can't transform lives.
>
> You can't touch people's hearts.
>
> You can't help raise the vibration of the planet.

As a woman in her late forties going through perimenopause, there's a whole other layer of invisibility and insecurities that appear at this stage in life.

It's easy to walk down the street and feel completely invisible and reminisce about the days when men smiled at you, or construction workers wolf-whistled! *(I know there's a whole separate issue here that we never talked about in the 80s and 90s, but for the purposes of this chapter, I'm focusing on being noticed, being seen, feeling attractive, feminine and sexy.)*

So, how do we reframe the rejection that comes with invisibility?

The fear of rejection (by others) is simply a reflection of the things we reject within ourselves, because of the stories we made up in our heads when we were young during situations where we didn't feel loved, acknowledged, seen or heard.

Therefore, we can offer ourselves the invitation to wholly accept who we are; all our physical, emotional and spiritual gifts, our unique personalities and innate brilliance.

Journal Prompts:

Take some time to explore your inner depths with these prompts for self-reflection and discovery.

- I feel rejected by [person's name or a certain situation] and this makes me feel [insert feelings].
- When or where do I feel invisible?
- How does that feel inside my body? Where do I feel sensations and what do they feel like? (E.g. a tightness in my throat, a clenching in my gut, the need to rush to the bathroom.)

> - Is any of this a repeating pattern? Are there feelings that come up frequently, or situations that happen over and over again?
>
> - What do you feel might be at the root of these feelings and behaviour patterns?

Reframing Rejection

A long time ago, I took a beginner's course in Emotional Freedom Technique (EFT), commonly known as 'Tapping'. It's a brilliant technique which I highly recommend you explore as it's a simple, discreet way to reframe negative thoughts or to regulate your nervous system in times of stress.

While tapping rhythmically on specific points of the hands, face and chest, you repeat a sentence that can be tailored to suit your exact needs in that moment. It goes something like this:

> **'Even though I feel** [rejected by my partner / invisible when I walk down the high street], **I deeply and completely love and accept myself.'**

I invite you to consider EFT as a gateway to shining a light within and starting to heal the energetic layers that are preventing you from living your best life.

NO GOOD AT GOODBYES

Things that keep us stuck:

- Hoarding and general clutter in our environments

- Not letting go of fears and negative emotions

- Holding onto physical possessions, including cards and letters

- Putting exes or dead relatives on a pedestal

For as long as I can remember, I've hated goodbyes. As a deeply sensitive, empathic child, letting go of anything wasn't easy. I've frequently explored the workings of my inner mind and energy blocks to figure out where in my childhood this emotion comes from.

One of my earliest memories is during a family caravan holiday in the countryside, just me and my parents. One evening, late at night, my mum was taken away in an ambulance. Two-year-old Lorraine was scared, confused and wanted her mummy back.

I don't know what I was told at the time, but years later I learned that my mum had had a miscarriage. As a toddler, I had no idea how to deal with the fears, sadness and anger I was struggling with and over the subsequent weeks, my behaviour changed and I would pretend to shoot anyone who came to our house with my hands and a 'bang bang' sound.

As a woman who's been on a journey of self-growth and healing for many years, I can only look back with compassion and love – both for the little girl who was scared and upset, and for my parents who handled the situation in the best way they knew at the time, with the communication tools they had.

I've shared already some thoughts about my fear of rejection and the sadness I felt in relationships when I didn't feel seen, heard or understood. And while there have been many sad goodbyes and endings in my life (and in yours too no doubt), there's a flip side to my personality that loves leaving old chapters behind and exploring the next stage with enthusiasm and excitement.

Being deeply connected to my intuition meant I always 'knew' when I was making the right choices, even when it meant leaving people or places behind.

At eighteen, I moved to France by myself to work for a year. At twenty-one, I left a long-term relationship and moved out of our shared house. At twenty-four, I switched careers and moved to a new country soon after. Later, I became a mother (twice), got divorced and changed career direction again!

I always put a lot of that down to my Gemini personality – having 'two sides' to me meant that I got bored easily and moved on.

(I'm only recently discovering that this pattern of obsession, boredom and always seeking the next exciting thing could also be linked to the dopamine-craving patterns of ADHD – which isn't actually attention deficit at all, but boredom when things are too easy and hyper-focus when something is interesting and stimulating. I resonate with much of the ADHD content shared online today and while I'm not intending to seek a diagnosis, this awareness helps me to explore and understand myself in new ways.)

I've also come to realise that much of the negative energy around goodbyes or positive energy around taking big leaps in life comes from a place of control.

In situations where you have control over the outcome, and you know in your heart and soul that it's the right thing to do, then everything feels 'right', even if it does involve ending a relationship or moving away from loved ones.

The hardest goodbyes are the ones where you have no control – like when our beautiful pets or loved ones die. Having lost many bunnies, guinea pigs and cats over the last thirty-five years, as well as two grandmothers, a soulmate friend and my father, I know first-hand how hard it is to let go, grieve and move on.

But just like in nature, something even more beautiful comes in to fill the void they left behind. My mum has blossomed into an independent, creative, community-focused woman now she has more time to herself and no one else to look after at home. And while I never thought I'd have another cat as amazing as the one I lost in 2011, I've gone on to have two more, each even more deeply connected to me and intuitive than the previous one. Every pet we've had has filled our hearts with joy and brought so much love into our lives.

The problem we have as humans (particularly in Western cultures) is that we cling on to everything with this energy of fear. As our pets or family members age, we begin to imagine life without them and instantly feel sad – both in our minds and our bodies.

But for every moment we spend worrying about a future event, we lose a moment of presence with our loved ones.

The same is true for mothers who get anxious and sad about their child starting school, or finishing school and moving to university or away from home for the first time.

The more tightly we cling onto our loved ones from this place of fear, the less able we are to drop into love and truly enjoy every moment we have together.

'If we're in fear, we're not in a place of love. When we're in a place of love, we can't be in a place of fear. Can you think of a time when you've been in both love and fear? It's impossible.'

– Elisabeth Kübler-Ross

Love and fear cannot coexist.

How can you gently release the suffocating grip of fear and sink into the energy of pure, unconditional love?

NOSTALGIC CLUTTER

As a child and young woman well into my thirties, I was an exceptionally sentimental human being holding onto so many items from the past that held some kind of special meaning: clothes, cuddly toys, photos, letters and cards, my children's early drawings and paintings, their first shoes…. You name it, I kept it (and still have a lot of it!).

I realised how much of a problem it was when I moved out of a house in 2013, just weeks after my fortieth birthday. Over the previous decade, I'd filled the spacious loft with all the 'stuff' I couldn't bear to part with; items that might one day be useful, had cost a lot of money or simply items that had sentimental ties.

It took six weeks, two skips, multiple trips to the charity shops and endless Facebook marketplace sales to clear the space!

I've since made a pact with myself to never use a loft space again! If it doesn't fit in my garage, cupboards or drawers then there isn't space for it! I try to only replace items rather than bring lots of new stuff into the house – especially when it comes to clothes, shoes, toiletries and kitchen items.

Journal Prompts:

- How do you feel about the 'stuff' in your home?

- Are you overwhelmed by clutter?

- Do you get stressed out every day trying to decide what to wear and ending up with a 'floordrobe'?

- How would it feel to clear space in your home?

- Do you feel ashamed by the amount of clutter or disorganisation there is in your home? (I've learnt this is another common ADHD symptom – check out the book *Dirty Laundry* by Richard Pink and Roxanne Emery, it's brilliant!)

- Is your kitchen a relaxing place to cook, or do overflowing cupboards make you avoid the area and choose simple options like takeaways or ready meals instead?

- Would you class yourself as nostalgic?

- Do you hold onto items for far too long? (Like keeping old love letters and photos from past relationships even when you've moved on and married the love of your life?)

- How would it feel to release these old items?

Top Tips for Letting Go:

- When clearing out old cupboards, boxes and drawers, allow yourself some time to reflect on why sentimental items mean so much to you. What is the energy you're holding onto? Is it love or fear?

- For physical personal items like children's drawings, handwritten cards or letters or photos, keep a select few in ONE special box, and take photos of the rest to store as digital files. They're much more accessible on your phone than packed away in a box and might even bring you more joy while releasing the stress of not having enough storage space!

- If you're holding onto clothes or other items that might have cost a lot of money and still be in excellent condition, it can be hard to let go because we still have an attachment to their financial worth. Donating thousands of pounds (dollars) worth of clothes to charity can feel gut-wrenching, particularly if you're not in a great financial position. But the truth is, that money was spent a long time ago and clearing space in your home will bring you so much joy and freedom from overwhelm. If you *can* sell items, of course try that first, but if you've got bags of clothes sitting around the house for months on end (or years!), then they need to go.

PART TWO

LEARNING TO FLY

STEPPING INTO THE UNKNOWN

It's going to be wild and messy.

What might it look like?
What might it feel like?
To go beyond your edges.
To let go.
To surrender to the wild abandon of the fires that burn
within.

Perhaps it would be like standing on the edge of a huge
black hole.
A deep canyon.
A high cliff.
And then taking a leap forward knowing that you may
never get out again.

That's why it's scary.
That's why we back off.

That's why we don't go there.

But what if that's where the magic happens?

What if that's where we're meant to go?

What if we'll find all the answers as we leap?

Let go.
Trust.

Embrace every wild adventure.
Let go of expectations.
Allow life to surprise you.

Have faith, beautiful soul.
It's all unfolding as naturally
and magnificently
as a rose coming into bloom.

EMBRACING VULNERABILITY

In September 2019, I broke my ankle whilst moving my daughter into her first-year university accommodation. With an insignificant slip on a damp pavement, a loud crack and an instant wave of nausea, something in the Universe shifted as much as the bones in my left ankle.

In the weeks that followed, stuck indoors with an inflatable boot, crutches and a never-ending creativity in how to make healthy food and carry it to the lounge while balanced on one leg, I decided I was ready to give up the struggle.

Breaking my ankle forced me to sit still, accept help and truly embrace my vulnerability.

It was as if everything had been leading up to that point.

- All those times I had decided to put other things ahead of self-care.

- All the times I'd put someone else's needs ahead of my own.

- All the times I hadn't stepped up and spoken my truth.

I decided in that moment that it was time to put *me* first again.

I knew it was time to nurture the beautiful soul within me and the human body that craved sensual touch, playful creativity and wild adventures.

I desperately wanted to hang out with the wild woman within me; the gorgeous goddess that held the key to my ability to truly savour everything this lifetime had to offer.

In essence, I was ready to let love into my life in every corner of my world and every facet of my being.

I had no idea *how* it was going to happen or what it was going to look like. But the intention was set. The Universe saw my commitment, so all I had to do was release expectation and trust that everything would fall into place…

CALLING IN SUPPORT

It didn't take long for me to realise that I might need support in calling in a great love. After all, I'd invested in support for other areas of my life and business, and allowed support in while my ankle was healing, so why not pay to have an expert on my side in the quest for love?

The Universe works fast when you're focused and clear on your goal.

Within a day or two, I saw a social media post for a new monthly membership group designed to support women seeking love – within themselves and within the dynamics of a healthy, intimate relationship. I already knew the coach, Katie Phillips, as an expert in the areas of love, dating and relationships, having listened to her speak at an event in Brighton a couple of years earlier. I jumped straight in, grabbing the free bonus materials before the group officially launched in January 2020.

Building relationships and finding connections with the other women was a beautiful experience and gave me a true sense of love and support.

It didn't even matter if 'my man' didn't show up because this group gave me the opportunity to feel into what I'd been missing: putting myself first and opening up to receive loving guidance on my quest for a soulmate partnership.

'If you want to fly,
give up everything that
weighs you down.'

– UNKNOWN

BEHIND THE MASK

My smile sometimes hides my true feelings.

Behind the happy, smiling, positive exterior has been a sadness I didn't realise was there, sitting heavily in my body, causing energy blocks that manifested into physical illness and challenging situations.

At some point, I realised that despite the fact I had been a prolific content creator since way before social media, websites and mobile phones, I wasn't really sharing the deep feelings that swirled around my mind and engulfed my body. Not online, nor in my closest relationships, and probably not even with myself!

The problem was, I didn't know what these feelings related to. I didn't know why they were there or how to describe them – let alone share them with others.

Along with the sadness, I carried the weight of my judgements around my own thoughts and feelings. Add that to a lifetime of always feeling like I was a little bit different to everyone else, and it's no wonder I chose to keep my 'weird and crazy' stuff hidden inside.

After joining a group coaching program, I realised that although I carried an inner sadness around personal events – like never truly allowing myself to grieve for my father – I was also exhausted and frustrated with the constant struggle against injustice. Injustice with big world events, and smaller injustices closer to home.

Our coach explained that frustration is a combination of anger and sadness. So rather than battling the emotion of frustration, we should look inward at the anger and the sadness.

In one particular 'hot seat' session, the coach asked me, *'How are you right now?'*

She could sense the sadness behind my vibrant energy, constant talking and big smile. She explained it was like the pressure that builds up against a dam. The key to releasing the sadness is, of course, to allow the dam to open and let the water flow…

She invited me to make peace with whatever happened in my life, and the stories I made up about certain events so that I could finally feel freedom from the pain within.

At the time, I wrote this in my journal…

| I'm going to break the dam and live my dream life.

When we look from the perspective of our story, we can only see what fits in the box.

Little Lorraine, how did she feel? How did she see the world?

None of it is WHO you are, it's just what you learnt.

I realised that covering up sadness had become part of my identity. And in turn, I attracted people into my life who I judged for keeping their feelings hidden or not being able to communicate deeply and intimately in the way I desired. They were literally a reflection of me – even though I couldn't see that at the time.

Going through the experience of this group coaching programme helped me to see myself as separate from my story. My aha moment was realising that even attracting certain people into my life is just my story. And as my story and I are separate, I can leave it behind.

Walk away and move on.

Invite in compassion, kindness and love for myself.

Be present with my feelings.

Allow myself to release the resistance I've been clinging on to and let others truly SEE me.

Ask myself questions that lead me into BEing my true self, free from the shackles of my own judgements, stories and limiting beliefs.

And remember,

It's OK to be the student, to not have it all figured out and to spend time in the messy parts of your life's journey, because…

'Life IS the messy parts.'

– From the movie *Letters to Juliet*

NO ONE IS COMING TO SAVE ME

Around the time I was recovering from my broken ankle and opening up to receive support from the Universe in terms of a romantic partner, I also decided it was time to let go of old versions of me that struggled with money and move forward with a new mindset. I said to myself:

What if it doesn't have to be this hard?

What if it gets to be *easy*?

As I reflected and journalled on all my thoughts, feelings and blocks around money (again! – I'd been working on money mindset and energetic blocks since first reading Denise Duffield Thomas's *Get Rich Lucky B*tch* book many years earlier), I realised that I was still holding onto an energetic block around people who don't have to take responsibility with money.

When something consistently irritates or triggers us it's always a reflection of our thoughts and beliefs.

And I realised that their stories aren't my story, and that no one is coming to save me...

At the time I wrote:

> Which means I have to take responsibility...
>
> For ALLL OF IT!
>
> The income
>
> The expenses
>
> The savings
>
> The clients
>
> The work
>
> The emotional, physical, spiritual and financial support
>
> The love
>
> The treats
>
> The romance
>
> I have to take responsibility for all that myself.

And when I do that, the Universe will naturally support me.

OK so how does that look?

What comes up?

The little girl in me wants to stamp her feet and say it's not fair.

But then life isn't fair.

We have to create our own success and happiness.

If I allow the little girl to live in scarcity mode of 'they have it and I don't' then I'll stay stuck here forever.

It's OK that you're where you are now.

It's OK that you didn't have certain things as a child.

I'm sorry you had to experience all the challenges and trauma in childhood that made you form the beliefs you have today.

I'm sorry you didn't feel loved, valued, appreciated.

I'm sorry you didn't feel worthy of luxurious gifts.

I'm sorry that you were expected to live with just the basics, with 'just enough'.

But that time is over now.

You're not a child anymore.

You're an adult with free will.

You have the power to create your own reality.

So, little girl,

What shall we create?

What shall we do?

Who shall we become?

Let the magic in. What if this gets to be exciting?
Magical even?

RELEASING ATTACHMENT

*'What was the point at which you
started to let go of the old versions of you?'*

I heard this question in a podcast and it really resonated.

As I looked back and reflected on my relationship break-ups, I realised that although I let each person go quite quickly, I had to spend the next few months (or years in one case!) letting go of the old version of me *and* my attachment to this old version of myself.

Boom! When I realised this, it was a powerful shift that enabled me to quantum leap into the next beautiful phase of my life.

Looking back throughout my whole life, I know that I've always been tuned into my intuition and inner guidance system, allowing that 'gut feeling' to propel me into the next chapter.

However, my ego and the unhealed parts of my psyche meant that I carried a deep wound of rejection and abandonment.

(Even if I was the one who initiated the break-up, there was still something in their behaviour or an event that made me believe I was being abandoned or rejected. And initiating the break-up is a way of either staying in control or pressing the self-sabotage button instead of having uncomfortable conversations.)

When the *Raising Wild Birds* concept first dropped into my mind in 2020, it coincided with a new relationship which was to go on to test my rejection issues over the following months before it finally ran its course. In that time, I journeyed deep inside myself, questioning everything about the way I'd previously behaved and communicated in relationships which ultimately led me to a deeper understanding of myself.

I learnt to trust myself more deeply, to honour where I was at and to let go of attachment from a place of love, not fear.

I had to let go of old ways of being, old belief systems, old habits and learn to drop into love. And to live every day from that place of love.

It wasn't always easy; the feeling of fear reared its ugly head (in the form of jealousy, fixing or withdrawing) many times, but I saw so much transformation in who I was, how I lived, and how I approached every moment of every day.

After the relationship ended a few months later, I knew it had been a pivotal point in my life, but what I didn't realise was how much more growth there was ahead for me. This was just the beginning!

It wasn't just letting one person go, it was letting an old version of me die so that a new one could be reborn.

The more I dropped into love, the easier it became.

As I journaled about the concept of setting wild birds free and not keeping them caged, I realised this was never about a man or a relationship, but a metaphor for my life and my personal growth.

It became crystal clear that I needed to embark on the same journey as a young bird: starting out as a fledgling – small but with an innate determination to learn to fly. As I'd begin to jump from one branch to the next, instinct would kick in and I'd spread my wings and take flight. Before long, I would be soaring high, flying across mountain peaks and seeing the world from a whole new perspective.

LIGHTEN THE ENERGETIC LOAD

Sometimes life on Earth feels hard.

And we humans are far better at criticising and judging ourselves than learning how to be gentle with our souls.

Instead, we numb the pain and discomfort through emotional eating, overworking, excessive exercise, alcohol, drugs, or simply shutting ourselves off from love and relationships in a quest to not experience even *more* pain.

It's time we learnt how to energetically lighten our load and to walk away from the things that don't serve our wellbeing, so that we have the energy to walk towards the things we *really* want.

This is something that took me a long time to truly anchor in and embody. It's easy to read about and mentally 'learn' what we need to do, but physically putting it into practice in every moment of every day takes a lot more effort and energy.

Learning to be gentle with yourself means you have to treat yourself like that precious, fragile baby bird – with love, compassion and kindness.

And you have to learn to create and enforce your own boundaries too.

Knowing when to say no and when to walk away from situations, people or opportunities is crucial.

A great question to ask yourself each day is:

How do I want to feel today? And what do I need to do, or who do I need to be, to make that happen?

Learning to take care of ourselves energetically is not something that's taught in school, and unless we have particularly spiritual parents, we don't learn this at home either. And yet, it's a fundamental principle of being able to thrive, not just survive.

So, how do we take care of ourselves energetically?

The first step is cultivating the awareness and understanding that we're so much more than the physical body we see in the mirror.

When I used to teach nutrition, I talked about the different elements of health, and how we need to have all of them in balance in order to be in 'optimum health'.

These are:

- **Physical health** – Through regular exercise and daily movement, good posture and a regular sleep pattern.

- **Emotional health** – Good relationships, a great support network, fresh air and sunlight all support our mental and emotional wellbeing.

- **Chemical health** – Our body's cellular make-up is supported by healthy food and negatively affected by toxins and chemicals in food, pharmaceuticals, the environment and products we use on our skin. We also know that stress plays a huge role in our health at a cellular level and is the cause of many diseases.

- **Spiritual health** – For some people, this is religion and community, for others it's time in nature or a connection to the inner self through journalling, crystals and tarot cards.

- **Energetic health** – Creating healthy boundaries plays a huge part in our energetic health. These can be with people or work, as well as parts of our lifestyle, the way we spend our time and saying 'no' to things that don't make us feel good.

Having studied this for many decades, professionally and through my own lived experience, I would now say that our emotional, energetic and spiritual health is as equally important as our physical and chemical health. *(Twenty years ago I would have said that nutrition sat in first place.)*

It's now been scientifically proven that loneliness shortens our lifespan, while having close relationships and a sense of community helps people to live longer, healthier, happier lives.

When we're lonely, unhappy or bored, we make poorer choices in all aspects of our lives. When we feel loved, safe and appreciated, we are more likely to make better choices that enhance our overall sense of wellbeing and contribute to our long-term goals.

In my own personal experience, I've noticed that when I'm in a new relationship or have another reason to feel excited and happy, I'm far more likely to go to the gym regularly, keep the house tidy, take better care of myself and wear brighter, more feminine clothes.

So, the question is, why do we feel the need to wait for these amazing (and sometimes rare) situations before taking better care of ourselves physically, mentally, chemically, spiritually and energetically?

What if we decided to look after ourselves first?

Wouldn't that create a more positive, vibrant and magnetic energy that would attract even more incredible people, opportunities and abundance into our lives?

SOFTEN YOUR HEART

One day, in my journalling ritual, I pulled an oracle card from Rebecca Campbell's *Starseed Oracle* deck that really resonated with the idea of loving yourself more. Some of the words in the oracle guidebook that particularly resonated with me included:

- *What's in the way of letting love in?*
- *Acknowledge the fears that are stopping you from letting love into your life.*
- *Find your way back to love.*
- *Soften your heart.*
- *How am I cutting myself off from love?*

Notes from My Journal:

This feels so aligned right now! I do have fears that are making me harder, that have made me put my barriers up. It's funny how I want certain people in my life to soften and be more physically loving but that's actually a reflection of how much I need to soften and open up to love.

I know I put up my walls very quickly. I've been hurt before so BOOM! Walls. Barriers. I have to accept the possibility that I may get hurt again in relationships, or that I may not always be liked or popular online. That's up to me to work through and release.

I have cut myself off from love in so many ways – physically, emotionally, financially, spiritually.

It's why I'm writing *Raising Wild Birds*, to share the concept that **learning to live from a place of love, not fear,** is an important part of our journey. The tough part is softening your heart and accepting you might get hurt, but allowing love in anyway.

Accepting that your business might not work out, or accepting that someone else wants to do things their way, even if you're watching from the sidelines, knowing intuitively that they're going to crash and burn – but that's their experience and their lesson to learn.

Do you use oracle cards or tarot? If you've never tried, I highly recommend giving them a go. They're a beautiful, gentle way to tap into your inner voice and nudge yourself in the right direction.

Some of my favourite decks include:

- Rebecca Campbell's *Starseed Oracle* and *Rose Oracle*
- Katie-Jane Wright's *Earth Alchemy Oracle*
- Denise Linn's *Nature Spirit Oracle Cards*

IT'S SAFE FOR ME TO SHINE

Read this affirmation aloud at least three times:

'It is safe for me to shine.'

How do you feel when you read this? What physical sensations arise in your body? What emotion feels strongest?

The first time I pulled this oracle card, it sparked reflection into some of my childhood experiences where I was shown it wasn't safe for me to shine.

For example, in secondary school, I remember being teased by other children for being clever ('square!'), for answering questions in school correctly, and for being praised by the teachers. I soon learned to dim my shine, to not always put my hand up and to pretend I didn't know the answers. Instead of being able to truly embrace the amazing feeling of receiving awards for great work, I felt embarrassed. These childhood interactions shaped who I became as an adult, never pushing to my edges or shining my brightest light in case I'd be ridiculed and have to feel that shame and embarrassment again.

I've met so many women through my work and social circles who also have this deep-rooted fear of stepping into the limelight and sharing their truth. They're afraid to be who they really are and stand up for what they believe in because of the experiences they went through as a younger woman or child. Unfortunately, when we suppress our deepest desires and our truth, we build resentment, frustration, anger or sadness inside. And that never ends well. Those negative emotions will always surface at some point in the future, somehow, somewhere.

When we begin to 'do the inner work' – whether that's like this with personal growth books, journalling, oracle cards and an amazing circle of beautiful souls around us, or as a form of therapy with a qualified and experienced therapist – it's like a light is instantly shone on the parts of us that we'd kept hidden. And sometimes it's not easy to go to those deep, dark places because it's scary. It's the unknown. And we're usually afraid of what might happen if we open up memories and experiences from the past.

But in my experience, there are always so many great things that happen as a result of us looking within, clearing old and stuck energy and creating freedom and space in our mind and body.

Realising that I'd not felt safe to shine as a child in school ignited a fire in me. I developed a fierce energy to *never* let that happen to my daughters. It made me want to ensure that my girls would always feel comfortable shining bright in school, or in any kind of artistic or sporty hobby they loved (and later as women in the workplace).

This led me to making specific choices about schools and education and even to homeschooling, which worked really well for my youngest daughter and me for three years up to age sixteen.

Journal Prompts:

- Can you think of a time in your life when shining bright as the beautiful, magical soul that you are did not feel safe?

- Where in your body are you holding onto this negative energy?

- What did not feeling safe to shine lead you to **doing** or **avoiding**? (E.g. it led me to a boring job in a bank instead of pursuing my dream to work in the theatre. Or, I run an online business but I avoid showing up on video because I'm scared of being judged.)

- Where do you avoid speaking your truth? What consequences does that have?

- Visualise feeling completely safe to shine; to show up as who you really are – complete with all the unique qualities that make you *you*. What are you doing / What does your life look like? How does it feel? (Take some time to really drop into this scenario and *feel* it in your body.)

- What insights can you take from this exercise into your life or work today to make positive changes?

OPEN UP TO RECEIVE LOVE

Notes from My Journal:

The moment I saw that the Universe was giving me what I asked for, I realised it was time for me to let go of old fears and to simply show up as the most natural, raw and primal combination of feminine energy, sexuality, sensuality and love.

Until I release old versions of me, I'll never be able to move forward and become who I'm meant to be; to step into my fullest potential.

The layers of protection must go.

I release the protection I've built around myself.

I am open to love and new experiences.

I am open to receive love and positive energy.

I notice so many moments of synchronicity – like when the flowers in my garden bloomed at exactly the same moment as a new relationship started to blossom.

It's time to release expectation and let go of fears, to embrace vulnerability and be open to new experiences.

I'm looking forward to being able to show up as the real me. To shed the layers of fears because they only create barriers for someone to love the real me. I am so grateful for this experience, this opportunity.

I made the decision at the end of last year to let go of the struggle and to evolve to a point where I was ready for a man. I kept saying in the past I wanted a partner but I was never really, truly ready.

I can let nature take its course, whatever that may be. I'm ready for love, support, adventure and tuning into the wildest, most natural and feminine version of me.

I open my heart to receive.

I'm ready to soften, open my heart and receive love and abundance.

Journal Prompts:

- Create a list of ways you'd love to receive love and pleasure.
- How can you fill your cup?
- How can you make yourself feel amazing?

LET YOURSELF BE LOVED

Can you open up and receive love, kindness and compassion when it's offered?

Or do you back off, hide away, go silent or retreat?

During 2020, I had multiple situations where I was given the opportunity to **learn how to receive.** There were moments where I was triggered by certain words, actions or behaviours and instantly started making up stories in my head. My instant reactions to those situations have varied – sometimes with instant emotional responses and other times simply retreating, but all stemmed from a place of fear.

Fears that I would be rejected, that I wasn't good enough or that I wouldn't be loved.

Having these fear-based emotional responses is perfectly normal, but they can cause a lot of problems within relationships and to our own mental and emotional health.

The key is learning to live from a place of unconditional love.

We need to show ourselves love and treat ourselves with love, compassion and kindness every day. How we do that will vary, but may include learning to quieten the negative voices in our heads, nourish our bodies with healthy food and take time out every day for activities that make us happy.

Within relationships, communication is key. But it's very easy for some of us to want to *fix* the other person; to offer solutions or to judge and suggest changes. The best way to communicate is through listening from a place of love: judgement-free and calm.

If your partner retreats, goes silent or reacts with an emotional outburst, it can be easy to also react from that place of fear. (That's generally how arguments start!) But instead, choosing in that moment to show them love – to offer a hug (in real life or in a GIF!), to let them know you're there if they want to talk or share how they're feeling, or some other random act of kindness that you know is especially meaningful for them.

It all comes down to love.

You may have done a lot of inner work on yourself to live from a place of love, but are you truly opening up to receive love from others?

If you're staying stuck in life, and some parts of your world seem difficult, challenging and never-changing, perhaps there's an opportunity to look within and practice *receiving love*, kindness and compassion from others; to feel it in your heart and allow yourself to be vulnerable.

THE CYCLE OF GROWTH

When I was a young woman, I lived in a constant state of judgement. I was either judging other people or feeling judged myself. My mind never stopped with its internal chatter, and it was exhausting!

Looking back, I can see how I've always been someone with an innate need to constantly learn, create, adapt, grow, shift, embody and integrate (even if I didn't have the terminology to express it in this way). And because of that determination to be forever in a state of change, I judged a lot of people who spent their whole lives in a fixed pattern and with a fixed mindset.

For example, there were people in my extended family and friendship circle who did the same things every week. They watched the same TV soap operas, ate the same meals and never ventured far beyond their hometown.

Even as a teenager, I couldn't understand how they could live this way without getting bored!

My own parents too were very set in their ways, eating the same foods each week, following the same routine every day and rarely creating their own pattern interrupt. But where my parents differed from some other families was their constant desire to learn and grow. They both came from humble, working-class families and worked hard to move away from the city to create a better life for themselves and their children. They took adult education classes and learnt new skills which they knew was the key to creating a better future.

> *'Education is the key that unlocks
> the golden door to freedom.'*
>
> *– George Washington Carver*

I can see now that my judgement of others was a reflection of the thing I was most scared of: *not growing!*

In fact, most often the things that trigger strong reactions in us are the very things that we need to look at within our own lives.

I was judging others because I was afraid of staying stuck; of not achieving my goals and not living my dream life.

Once I realised that it didn't matter what anyone else did or said, and that I was free to carve my own path through this magnificent human existence, everything shifted.

I was finally free of the chains that kept me tied into negative behaviour patterns and my own limiting beliefs.

With this freedom came a sense of calm and stillness within. I no longer needed the mental chatter that kept my mind racing at 100mph day and night.

Letting go created space.

Space to devote to my own wellbeing, dreams and desires.

Space to live life in the present moment.

Space to simply be.

JUDGEMENTS AROUND RECEIVING

Where in your life have you placed judgements around receiving love, gifts or other things, and how did this cause you to react?

Delving into this question took me back to all the times I received gifts that didn't make me feel valued, special or understood.

As I journalled, I noticed I sounded like a spoilt brat at times, which was interesting, but that lit a fire in my belly that made me see that while I knew I *should* be grateful, I must always value my worth.

I realised how much all these childhood and young adult experiences have shaped how I value myself in adult life.

I've uncovered a lot of these feelings multiple times on money mindset work over the past decade, but something new always appears – which is why this work is never 'done'!

After a childhood filled with items that were generous and always gifted with love but never luxurious or expensive, I went a bit crazy with overdrafts, store cards and loans in my twenties which I can see was simply an attempt to match the material world around me to what I felt inherently I was worth. It wasn't all clothes and shoes, I also deeply valued international travel (something we'd never done as a family), new experiences and education.

In my late thirties, finances became an issue as I ended up a single parent living on an expensive island and working freelance on a part-time basis in order to be there for my daughters around their school days.

Looking back, it was easy to see how much more I'd become like my parents – living on very little, learning to budget, not giving the gifts I would love to give other people simply because the money wasn't there, not investing in myself or gifting myself treats or luxuries.

Some of this residual energy is still there, hanging around in my cells energetically and preventing me from living my best life and being paid what I'm truly worth for the work I do, and being open to receiving the 'gifts' I deserve to receive.

(It's interesting that 'receiving gifts' is my lowest score of the five love languages[1]. I value quality time and physical touch the most. This 'love languages' rabbit hole opened up a whole new layer of investigation, deep conversations and healing.)

---

[1] See *5lovelanguages.com* for more info on love languages.

Whilst journalling around the question at the start of this chapter, I arrived at a moment of profound realisation:

I was 'taught' (role modelled) that you said thank you and acted grateful even if you didn't like a gift or if it didn't 'feel' worthy of deep gratitude. Therefore, I have a learned practice and behaviour of accepting gifts, situations or behaviours that didn't match my worth or value. I.e. I've always been willing to accept something that didn't feel good to me, or truly 'enough'.

Of course, our parents come from a different generation. Those born shortly after WWII genuinely had very little and probably did feel incredibly grateful for even a satsuma in their Christmas stocking!

As I contemplated this, I wondered whether they too felt like they deserved more. And so the energy is carried on through every generation until someone changes the pattern and creates a new story for the future.

I know that my parents did everything they could to ensure my brother and I had a lovely childhood, and I am incredibly grateful to them and for the experiences I had. It's much easier to feel gratitude and love towards our parents and our childhood experiences once we've done the deep inner work and healing to let go of our own negative blocks, subconscious behaviours and unhealthy patterns or beliefs.

Journal Prompts:

- What judgements do you hold around receiving gifts or love?

- How many times have you received a gift that didn't feel energetically aligned? How did it make you feel? What would you have loved instead?

- Is there someone in your life whose love you'd really like to receive more fully? How would you like that to look and feel?

- Are you happy with the gifts or love you give others? What would you like to do differently? Why? How would that make you feel?

PART THREE

SOARING HIGH

A DESIRE-LED LIFE

It's impossible to live a whole, wild, fulfilled life without tuning into our desires.

But do we even know what our true desires are?

Unless we give ourselves the space and time to dig deep into our heart and soul, and the parts of our truth we keep hidden, how will we ever even know what we truly, deeply want?

If you're anything like me, you can probably recall many occasions where you've 'gone with the flow' and ended up spending the day, or an evening, or even an entire holiday(!) doing what someone else wanted to do. Maybe you gave in to keep the peace, or perhaps you just didn't have any better ideas at the time, or maybe (and far more insidious) you were too afraid to speak your truth.

As I've got older and really begun to understand who I am, what lights me up and what drains me, I find it easier to create loving boundaries or speak up in these kinds of 'what shall we do?' scenarios.

So, back to the burning question…

What do I truly desire?

I'm going to share some of my desires here, and I invite you to take some time to create your own list. Keep your notebook handy at all times to add to the list, or to delete things when you realise that they're not really *your* desire at all, just something you think you *should* be wanting to do!

- I desire to feel safe and loved.

- I want to spend time with people who soothe my nervous system or excite and inspire me.

- I desire excitement in my life – the kind that gives me tingles!

- I desire to 'work' almost entirely in my zone of genius so that every day feels like a fun adventure, not a job.

- I desire to spend at least two months every year in a foreign country as a local, not a tourist – living in a house or apartment rather than a hotel. I want to learn new languages, see places through different lenses and explore new ways of living and being that can enhance my own life back home.

- I desire a long-term relationship based on real friend-ship, shared values, intimacy and an expansive, growth mindset.

- I want to continue learning throughout my entire life – to 100 years young and beyond! I want to learn new languages so that I can talk with and listen to people from different backgrounds and cultures. I want to keep up with technology so that I never lose touch with the modern way of life and I want to study seemingly random subjects that appear in my life and fill me with excitement!

- I desire to put down roots in one place; to own a beautiful property that has space to grow over the years and is filled with light and with a beautiful view. I desire a large vegetable garden, an orchard, a kitchen herb garden, and lots of different spaces to sit at different times of day to take advantage of the sunshine, nature, light and shade.

Desire Affirmations

Once you have your desires list, you can turn each statement into positive desire affirmations. (These are mine.)

- I am safe and loved.

- I attract people who soothe my nervous system and calm my soul.

- I attract people who activate, inspire and motivate me.

- I create my own excitement and magical experiences every day.

- I align my work with my truth, my values and my heart. Everything I do is an extension of who I am BEing.

- I create my own opportunities.

- The more I live my truth and love who I am, the more effortlessly I attract the right soulmate partner.

- The more I immerse myself in what I love, the more opportunities flow to me.

- My presence and joy bring me a constant flow of abundance, good health and prosperity.

- Every day I make a difference simply by being present and being me.

- I am a lightworker and people are drawn to me.

- I am in a state of effortless flow and creativity every moment of every day.

- I cherish every moment and feel gratitude for even the smallest things.

- I am open and ready to be led in the direction of my dreams.

Thank you Universe, guardian angels, ancestors and spirit guides.

And so it is.

CREATING SPACE FOR YOUR DESIRES

Over the last twenty years, we've become immersed in a world of fast-paced communication and instant gratification on devices that have become smaller and smaller and are typically in our pockets or close to us almost 24/7! It's overwhelming, exhausting, stressful and bad for our physical and mental health.

After the highs and lows of 2020, I knew instinctively that I was spending far too much time consuming content and needed to create space physically, emotionally and digitally in my life in order to be able to achieve my goals and attract more incredible abundance, love and relationships into my life.

I'd begun to notice I was more easily triggered, my energy was all over the place, my natural happy, positive state was replaced with low feelings that I'd never experienced before. Being so easily 'knocked off kilter' each day meant

I wasn't living the life I wanted to be living and making very little progress towards achieving my goals (like writing this book!).

In my journal, I wrote:

> Create space, Lorraine. Create space for your beautiful life to fill you with the kind of immense joy and love you deserve.
>
> Create space to be loved wholeheartedly.
>
> Create space for magical things to appear.
>
> Create space to truly live the wild adventures you desire...

CREATE SPACE

DELIBERATE INTENTION

At some point in the last few years, the word 'intentional' kept appearing in my life, which got me thinking about being intentional with our time and with our lives.

This was closely followed by the word 'deliberately' on someone's Instagram story and I thought 'YES, that's it! It's all about being very deliberate about what I do and how I spend my time.'

I always pay attention when the Universe shows me the same sign repeatedly – like a word, a person, a place, a feeling or an object. This is a beautiful way for us humans to experience the universal magic of synchronicity.

The dictionary definition of 'deliberately' is: *Done consciously and intentionally.*

I realised that this described beautifully my theme (or word) for 2021. To consciously and intentionally choose how I spend my time and my energy. And to do that with grace and gratitude.

Which led me to thinking about all the times I've said I'm 'doing' self-care but in reality I'm multi-tasking. Like taking a bath and watching a YouTube video or movie, or reading a book but texting someone at the same time, or cooking dinner while listening to a podcast, or watching TV and scrolling through Twitter or Pinterest.

(Hopefully you're not multi-tasking as you read this! If you are, step away from this book and your TV/phone and get outside in nature or do some dance, movement or stretching.)

And so, I began to consciously do ONE thing at a time.

At first, I didn't succeed every single time, but on the whole, I managed it well, which gave the impression of having 50% more hours in the day and also feeling more happy with what I achieved; more contented and even a little smug!

It's something I've continued to come back to every few months, along with actively creating space through regular decluttering of my physical, digital and emotional space.

Deliberately, consciously, intentionally and with grace and gratitude.

- *How does that sound to you?*
- *Does it resonate?*

- *Where could you be more intentional or deliberate with your actions?*

- *How could you act (or react) with more grace and gratitude?*

REFRAMING THE STRUGGLE

For many years, since diving deeply into personal growth work, I'd become accustomed to saying, 'I'm ready to give up the struggle'. But what I really meant was: I want things to be different (around love and money) but I'm not quite willing to let go of who I am and the things I'm attached to in order to truly shift the dynamic and open up to a new way of being.

Struggle had become just another identity label that I'd attached to myself.

Constantly using the word 'struggle' – whether in conversations or simply in my own head – was reinforcing the fact that struggle remained in my life! Because it was always there, nothing changed. Our minds are pretty good at keeping us stuck but once you have that lightbulb moment of awareness, *that's* the point at which things really begin to change, shift and transform.

One big breakthrough I had was realising that when I journalled about the future version of me, I often focused on the 'absence' of something negative rather than the 'presence' of something positive. For example, 'I want a life free of tummy pain, or free from money struggles'.

It sounds positive, but the Universe only hears the words 'pain and struggle' and gives you more of that!

A better way of wording it would be:

- I want a healthy, active body that allows me to go on long hikes and lift heavy weights.

- I want more than enough money all the time to pay my bills and live a comfortable life as well as for all the little luxuries and experiences that make me a happier and more generous person.

I decided to reframe 'giving up the struggle', as you'll see in these extracts from my journal musings:

What will giving up the struggle look like?

It looks like more money in the bank and more financial security.

It looks like regular exercise and a healthy recovery rate, not constant tiredness.

It looks like creativity and flow rather than stuckness and 'ugh' energy.

It looks like feeling supported rather than doing everything alone.

It looks like feeling safe and secure, not constantly in a state of high alert.

It looks like an abundance of healthy food and all the ingredients to make tasty meals, rather than always making do and eating rice and beans or leftovers.

How does giving up the struggle feel?

It feels lighter. There's a lightness in my step and in my energy.

My body feels younger, more youthful, more energetic.

I desire to get outside and exercise because I know it won't drain my physical or mental energy.

I will have no more fear around tiredness and fatigue post-exercise and won't let it stop me doing what I really want.

I feel excited about life and about each day.

I feel excited to do things – whether they're personal, physical, with friends or for business.

I feel colourful and vibrant.

I feel more flowing energy and creativity.

I feel more able to focus and give things my full attention.

I feel have more clarity and a clear vision of the future.

How can I reword 'giving up the struggle'?

I'm living my best life in all ways.

I'm living my healthiest life, my most abundant life, my most joy-filled life, my happiest life, my sexiest life, my most curious and my most creative life.

Take some time to reflect on any negative forms of expression you use regularly and how you can flip the script.

(Note: This is not about masking pain and sadness with positivity, but becoming aware of your inner voice and how it might be impacting your happiness and creativity.)

LIVING YOUR BEST LIFE

If you're reading this book, chances are pretty high that you've come across 'dream life' visualisations and exercises before.

I love doing this exercise every few months and am usually drawn to do so by planetary and lunar shifts that bring about a transformative energy. I feel it in every cell in my body.

I start to get fizzy feelings, like butterflies, excited antici-pation and that first school crush all mixed in together! I'm usually super creative at these times and seem to write new e-books in just a few hours or completely shift my services and offers. It's like I know I'm on the cusp of a new level of living and being and have to anchor in that energy into a visual, tangible form.

These journal prompts will guide you as you tap into your best life. You can write, draw, photograph, create a collage or do anything creative that fills you with joy. This should be a fun experience, so go with the natural flow of energy from within and listen to the gentle whispers from your soul and the serendipitous nudges from the Universe.

Once the activity feels complete, ground yourself by coming back to Earth with a mundane task (like emptying the dishwasher or folding laundry) or going for a short walk in nature, dancing to your favourite song or taking a shower.

Keep some part of your drawings or notes visible over the coming weeks so you can continue to tap into this potent energy.

(I love it when I find my lists and doodles in notepads years later and realise that I made everything come true!)

Journal Prompts:

- What does my best life look like?
  How does it feel?

- What does an ideal day in my
  best life look like? How does it feel?

- What do I look like in my best life?
  What do my surroundings look like?

- How do I feel living my best life?
  What do I love to do every day?

- What energy do I radiate living
  my best life?

- Who are the people around me?
  How does it feel being with them?

- What would the best-life version
  of me tell the current version of me?

SOUL SISTER CONVERSATIONS

'Knowledge speaks, but wisdom listens.'

– Jimi Hendrix

Some of my biggest shifts have come through conversations with my soul sisters who've come into my life for a season, a reason or a lifetime. We've dedicated time to each other. We've listened. We've shared our thoughts. It's a beautiful uplifting energetic exchange.

Paying for a coach has its place, but making time for your soul sisters and nurturing these relationships is magical.

Making time for people is making time for yourself. For your growth and expansion.

'When you talk, you are only repeating what you already know.
But if you listen, you may learn something new.'

– Dalai Lama

In the corporate world, you might have regular chats with your mentor, or meet inspiring female entrepreneurs and CEOs at corporate events or lunches. Being surrounded by people who inspire and motivate you to step into your potential is an essential part of the personal growth journey.

When one of my soul sisters and I are going through a period of intense growth, like after a relationship break-up, pushing through financial struggles or at the exciting start of a new project launch, we set up weekly accountability gatherings via Zoom (or in person) for a few weeks. We both share how we're feeling, the challenges we're facing, the areas where we need to focus and our goals. The other person simply listens and holds space. No one tries to fix or offer solutions unless it's asked for. I've found this to be incredibly beneficial and we always end up feeling far more productive, creative, in-flow and abundant than when we try to go it alone.

If you're not comfortable opening up to other women, look inward and reflect on why that might be. Many women still carry an ancestral wound from the era of the witch trials hundreds of years ago where we were forced to turn on our sisters in order to stay alive.

If you don't yet have a close circle of loving, compassionate, inspiring female friends, make it your mission to reach out to connect. Try Facebook groups, membership groups, local activity groups or group coaching programmes.

In our post-pandemic world, it seems to me like more and more people are drawn to meeting up in person – maybe going for a walk or having a cup of tea in a relaxed cafe.

I make the effort to nurture relationships with the women I already know, and to reach out to like-minded women locally or online to connect and see what magic might arise from our sisterhood chats.

Journal Prompts:

- Do you have a close circle of female friends?
- How could you deepen these connections?
- What's your preferred way to meet or talk to other women?
- How might it feel to step out of your comfort zone and meet in a new environment or with new people who you deem to be 'more successful' than you?

CREATING CONNECTIONS

I've always been aware of patterns and connections, knowing intuitively when two or more things (or people) fit together perfectly.

Which makes it all the more obvious to me when a connection is missing...

A couple of years ago I went to a sound healing 'gong bath' session which I had hoped would be a beautiful experience. Unfortunately, the leader didn't bring us together in a circle, or create any kind of cohesion between us. While the sound experience itself was nice, I came away feeling like it lacked a certain something.

Which made me contemplate how I bring people together – not solely for my own benefit but for the collective.

Soon after, I watched a YouTube video of a 'goddess gathering' which made me deeply desperately crave a similar style of soul-sister connection and togetherness.

And recently, I read about the concept of 'friendship days' which presented me the opportunity to reflect on the fact that we don't give our friendships the time and space to truly bloom and grow. Many of us are guilty of squeezing friends and family into our busy schedule – often between lots of things we don't even enjoy but feel we can't say no to!

What if we all made more effort to spend time together, or to spend a longer period of time with one friend?

How about a whole day out?

A visit to an art gallery or museum, a delicious lunch or coffee and croissants, a cosy afternoon in the cinema in winter or walking on the beach in summer, before heading home to cook plant-based food together and enjoy a quiet evening reading in each other's company or watching a movie or playing board games.

Perhaps I'm a little romantic but I'd love to create and nurture those kinds of deep and intimate feminine relationships.

And what about the other connections in our lives? The ones that are connected with our work, our hobbies or our personal growth.

During the pandemic lockdowns in 2020 and 2021, the word 'Zoom' suddenly became synonymous with meetings of all kinds, opening up a whole new space for gatherings that meant people could connect across different geographical locations.

Initially, people jumped at the chance to stay connected, but soon 'Zoom fatigue' kicked in, especially amongst those who had to use video calls for their remote work for twenty-plus hours every week!

Now, just a few years on, most people I meet are enthusiastic to return to in-person meetings and events, relishing the opportunity to be able to tune into body language and follow conversations without being distracted by the image of themselves on screen!

Being together in person means we can engage more of our senses. Hugging the friend who's going through a difficult time, shaking hands with the potential business partner, sharing food and drink taste experiences, experiencing special events like fireworks on New Year's Eve or crossing the finish line of the marathon.

Human beings *need* these in-person connections to truly thrive. As I mentioned earlier, it's even been shown that loneliness and social isolation have a severely negative impact on quality of life and longevity. It's probably playing a role in the huge rise in depression, anxiety and mental health issues across all age groups too.

So whether you're a self-confessed extrovert who jumps at the chance of heading to a party, or a quiet introvert who needs a lot of peaceful 'alone' time, our human connections are incredibly valuable. Nurturing our relationships is something we'll never regret.

What do you think?

How do you feel about your relationships, and what would you like to do differently?

WHO AM I?

Beyond the labels and identity,
I am nothing and everything.

Insignificant yet potent.

Who I am to me
is different to who I am to you,
to my children,
to my partner,
to my friends,
to my family,
to my clients.

Each one of us views life through a different lens.
A different perspective.

Mostly unaware of our magic.
Our potency.
Our brilliance.

Who am I?

A question so profound
and yet so simple.

REFRAMING REJECTION

The fear of rejection is simply a reflection of the things we reject in ourselves.

Why? Because of the story we made up in our heads as innocent babies and children when we first felt rejected.

The emotion of rejection is a beautiful invitation to wholly accept who we are: all our physical, emotional and spiritual gifts. Our brilliance, magnificence and potency.

Over the last few years, I've really dived into my own mind, heart and soul to figure out why I'm triggered into an emotion of rejection in a particular moment. I sit with the feelings of fear in my body, replaying all those stories of rejection from my lifetime. And then I ask myself how I can see this from a more loving perspective.

Of course, it's natural that relationships, friendships and jobs all come to an end and chapters close. Even if we're to blame on some level, rejection is simply a made-up story that allows us to stay stuck in our ego. Our Western culture loves a good victim story, so it's easy to feel like we fit in when we express our experiences in the way of 'something happening to us'.

It takes a stronger person to let go of fear and sink into love.

And to realise that these events happen *for* us.

There were times in my life where I allowed the painful emotions of rejection to spiral out of control, causing me to get angry, lash out verbally and say and do things I later regretted.

If I knew then what I know now, I wonder how different my life would look.

But of course, it doesn't work like that! Life is one big rollercoaster; an endless stream of highs and lows, learning points, failures and successes. We're meant to fall down and get back up, over and over again. Without those triggers, melt-downs and stressful or heartbreaking situations, we'd never have the impetus to transform and evolve.

- How does the emotion of rejection manifest for you?

- Do you still react the same way now as you did ten or twenty years ago, or has something shifted?

- Do you react from a place of fear? Or do you take time to compose yourself before showing up from a place of love?

When you feel rejection, it can be useful to use the EFT language and tapping technique:

> *Even though I am feeling rejected because [insert a brief description of the situation], I deeply and completely love and accept myself.*

_____

Affirmation:

I wholly accept myself, I am enough, I am loved.

GET CLEAR ON WHAT YOU DON'T WANT

I've already written about our desires and how we can tap into the things we really want in our lives. But it's also incredibly useful to know what we do NOT want!

When we're clear on the types of people, situations and 'stuff' that we don't want in our lives, it makes creating loving boundaries so much easier!

Now it's time for you to tap into your core values and inner truth and explore the things you would prefer to not have in your life. This helps you to gain complete clarity and spend more time focusing on what really means the most to you and will support you in moving your life forward.

Journal Prompts:

- What don't you want?

Try splitting this up into categories: work, love, money, home, social life or friendships.

- What do you know is a big NO for you? (The BIG non-negotiables)

For example: (Practical) I don't want to be stuck in a 9-5 corporate job for forty years. (Energetic) I don't want to work with people who don't light me up. (Financial) I don't want to work with people who don't see the value in what I do, or who consistently pay late or default on their payments. (Love) I don't want to be with someone who has a fixed mindset and won't grow with me.

- When it comes to health and physical wellbeing, what is a NO for you?

For example: I don't want to waste weekends in pubs and bars. I don't want to waste so many days of my life with a hangover. I don't want to be unhealthy, inactive and develop preventable diseases like others in my family. I don't want my lifestyle to negatively impact others or the planet.

- In love and relationships, what is a big NO for you?

For example: I don't want to be with someone who doesn't want to grow and evolve; someone who watches TV or goes to the pub every day and never has deep conversations with me. I don't want to be with someone who doesn't value their health and fitness.

- In work, career or running your own business, what is a NO for you?

For example: I don't want to feel undervalued, underpaid, taken advantage of, unmotivated or unsupported.

YOUR SOUL CRAVES MORE

It's crazy to think that I've spent so much of my life playing small, fitting in, going along with what others want and not openly speaking my truth.

And if I feel like this, I'm pretty certain you might do too.

I don't know if it's just our cultural conditioning, but whenever I write a list of 'desires', they're usually the culturally acceptable ones – like a fitter, healthier body, a nicer house, more money, a 'perfect' partner or more travel experiences.

But what about our real desires?

Why do we hold back from being honest about the things that would make us feel so deeply seen and utterly ALIVE?

I think it's about time that we flipped the script and started being honest to ourselves about what we really want.

Journal Prompts:

- Why don't I allow myself to take up more space?

- Why am I holding back?

- What might happen if I showed up as the brightest, boldest, and most real, raw and messy version of me?

- What does the 'taking up more space' version of me look like?

Here's a snippet from one of my desire-led journal entries:

> She goes after what she desires.
>
> What her soul craves. What her body desires.
>
> She wants volcanoes and earthquakes and tsunamis.
>
> She's not going to settle for a boring house on a street of identical houses.
>
> She's not going to accept an 'ok' love life.
>
> She wants it all.

She wants deep, messy love.

She wants unexplainable, can't-live-without-you love.

She wants sweat and tears.

She wants close faces and passionate kisses.

She wants early morning hikes to watch sunrise from the mountain top.

She wants deep conversations and tender touches.

She wants wild adventures, spontaneous embraces and nights under the stars.

She wants fire.

She wants moonlight on her body as he kisses her neck.

She wants handfuls of heaven and mouthfuls of magic.

Or, as Carrie says in the final season of *Sex and The City:* 'I'm someone who is looking for love. Real love. Ridiculous, inconvenient, consuming, can't-live-without-each-other love.'

RAINER AND LARA

Over all the years I've been actively working on my personal growth, releasing inner blocks, shifting energy and letting go of limiting beliefs, I've noticed that there have been periods where I deeply embody my empowered feminine energy, and periods where I embody my empowered masculine energy.

I'm highly aware of how different this feels to the years I spent in my disempowered masculine and feminine energies as a teenager and young woman. This showed up in traits such as impatience, a need for control (including only eating 'clean' food), risk-taking, anger, low confidence, low self-worth, perfectionism and fear of vulnerability.

It really wasn't until my forties that I realised I'd spent my whole life acting like a child because I'd never connected with, loved or honoured my inner child. Deep inside was a wounded little girl who just wanted to be seen, heard and understood. A girl who wanted to be hugged and loved, not judged and criticised (by others or by herself).

Reconnecting to and embodying my inner feminine energy was a beautiful experience. It brought me a deeper connection with sensuality, spirituality and nature. It gifted me beautiful bonds with like-minded sisters from all around the world. It took me on a whole new tangent with my business, focusing on copywriting for heart-centred, soul-led entrepreneurs, visionaries and leaders. It led me back to a more feminine way of dressing, embracing long floaty dresses and silky fabrics rather than wearing jeans every day!

Connecting with my empowered masculine energy was a different story though...

When you don't see amazing women thriving in their healthy masculine energy represented in the media growing up, it's hard to know what this looks and feels like – both in a physical male body and within us as women. *(We all have masculine and feminine energy within us regardless of our gender at birth.)*

The 80s, 90s and early 2000s were also an era where feminists were portrayed negatively as 'man-haters', mothers who went back to work were branded 'unfeminine' and the cause of the family unit breakdown, and if a woman made it to the top in the corporate world it was implied she slept her way there, while beautiful women who made it as supermodels were deemed to be 'stupid' because how could you possibly have looks *and* brains?! As a woman, you really couldn't win!

Of course, the truth is we can *all* have it all! We can look good on the outside and feel good on the inside. We can have financial and career success and happy relationships. So why does it still feel like we're somehow greedy for wanting it all?

In my research and learning around money mindset, particularly for those of us who have struggled with charging our worth as small business owners, I came across this concept that really stuck in my mind:

If you're a good person with a good heart who does good things, then having more money (or incredible wealth) will only amplify those qualities. You're more likely to be someone who is even more generous, using your money to do great things that help a lot of people.

In contrast, if you're the type of person who could be classed as 'bad', then your negative qualities of greed or selfishness will be magnified with an increase in wealth and you're more likely to spend selfishly and feel an obligation to help others rather than want to do it with love, generosity and kindness.

A big part of my journey getting to know and love my inner masculine energy has been around finances, wealth building and money management.

In my journalling, I asked myself:

> **What might creating my own financial security feel like?**
>
> *Peace of mind, strength, empowerment. I've got me.*

I realised that if I acknowledged and loved my empowered masculine, this energy would get stronger and I would feel happier, more valued, respected and loved.

If I treated my inner masculine energy with love, space and freedom to grow then this would also be reflected on the outside in how I showed up in all aspects of life, and in who and what I attracted in.

I could see how much my past actions, thoughts and patterns had suppressed parts of my inner masculine and how I was now ready to grow, fly and soar high above the mountains.

It was this realisation that coincided with the early concept of *Raising Wild Birds*. For a short while, I considered writing this book as a fiction novel, using the male and female lead characters to represent my inner masculine and feminine energies which would be woven through the storyline. *(I soon realised I'm not yet a talented fiction writer!)*

Rainer, my lead male character, would radiate the desirable traits of healthy, empowered masculine energy.

I had fun playing with this...

Rainer is the mountain climber. He's the one with the determination, energy and devotion to see things through.

He's the one with the full survival kit and the strong, fit body. When Rainer is out on the mountains he's at his best. He's in nature and moving his body. Pushing and testing his limits and stepping out of his comfort zone.

Rainer is also happy when he's playing with numbers, building wealth and seeing the results of his efforts pay off financially.

He loves writing too. He writes books that connect people to their inner warrior spirit and empowered masculine.

Rainer is happy when he's in the garden growing vegetables and fruit, or mowing the lawn, tending to plants and creating a sanctuary for him and his family.

Meanwhile, my inner empowered feminine character, Lara was a beautiful, sweet-natured soul:

Lara is a sensual creature who loves to be held and touched and to hug or be physically close to others. She loves to fly and be carried away. She is nurturing, nourishing, loving, kind, compassionate and a gentle soul who loves butterflies, bees and all animals and insects. She loves flowers, roses and smelling sweet scents.

She has an animal-whispering gift and connects on a different level with creatures of all shapes and sizes. She loves losing time indulging in a book, nature or with special people with whom she feels a great connection.

She loves being in flow; moving her body to music, singing, being close to water, watching the waves roll in. She is creative and artistic, loving to doodle and draw. She's drawn to cartoon character faces, symbols and languages. She loves to feel feminine in her body in floaty clothes, pretty shoes, luxurious fabrics and dainty jewellery.

(And yes, you might have guessed that there is a lot of me and my ideal romantic partner in those two descriptions… it's all part of manifesting my dream life!)

FINDING PLEASURE

I am potent. I am vulnerable. I am love.

What brings you pleasure?

Beautiful, unadulterated, blissful pleasure.

Is it that first sip of coffee in the morning? The way your dog rushes to greet you when you get home? The rush of excitement as the plane speeds down the runway before take-off? Sinking into a deep, hot bubble bath after a busy day at work?

As a child, I had no problem finding pleasure in the simplest of things: laying back on the soft grass watching the clouds float and morph into animal shapes across the sky; making daisy chains while watching the bees and butterflies on the dainty purple Buddleia flowers; eating cola flavoured 'Mr Freeze' ice poles on the swings in the park with friends.

On the surface, it might sound like we humans are great at filling our lives with pleasure, but the reality is that most people and families in busy Western societies are stuck in survival mode.

Surviving, not thriving.

When I devoted time to reflect on the concept of 'pleasure in my childhood' using a visualisation technique, I was able to see the bigger picture beyond the happy memories which led me to some deep realisations and aha moments.

I realised that I was never able to embody the *fullest* expression of me. I was the stereotypical 'good girl'. The one who did as she was told, followed rules, got good grades and (mostly) came home on time as a teenager.

In living life as a good girl, I suppressed my true desires. I squished myself into a neatly identifiable good girl box and got on with life.

Throughout my childhood, I was never exposed to adults indulging their desires or living a luxurious life. Everyone around me seemed happy enough in their life; seemingly content with a couple of weeks' holiday each summer, evenings on the sofa watching television and weekends seeing friends or extended family. In hindsight, family life in the 1970s and 80s seems far more simple than life today. Less choice and more satisfaction perhaps?

As a teenager, I started to see life differently from the adults around me (*it's an interesting scientific fact that teenagers are hardwired to be selfish and be focused entirely on things for their own benefit)* and began a continuous inner dialogue of criticism and judgement against those around me. No one was ever good enough and those that were just made me jealous!

In my own 'good girl' ways, I rebelled against the way of life I'd known for eighteen years and began to indulge in all kinds of beauty products, clothes, shoes and – most importantly to me – travel.

Each time I went to get highlights in my hair at the luxury salon that offered free Martini cocktails, I felt like I was living a life of luxury and I *knew* I deserved it! I knew I was worthy of these feelings of pleasure and I knew the value of spending money on the things that mattered.

Of course, becoming a young working adult in the early 1990s meant I quickly fell into the trappings of con-sumerism and managed to collect a purse-full of high street store cards that led me into a period of credit card and overdraft debt.

However, a lot of that indulgence, including sexually, came from a place of imbalanced, disempowered mascu-line energy.

Now I understand that pleasure and inner peace are interlinked.

Sensual pleasure, sexual pleasure, pleasure in freedom, nature, treating yourself with love and kindness, laughing, wild adventures, watching a sunset, birdsong at sunrise, bees and butterflies, cat cuddles, or the anticipation of new food and drink taste sensations.

Sensuality – as in bringing pleasure to the senses – is something we all crave on a daily basis. But we're also all guilty of not allowing ourselves to experience the bliss we really want.

For example, we might keep buying more jumpers (sweaters) because what we really want is one that *feels* incredible on our skin. Soft to the touch. Not itchy, scratchy or synthetic. But instead, we make do with the not-so-soft jumpers because they're all that's available or in our price range but they never truly fulfil the need for sensuality we desire.

Or, we might be walking in the countryside and really want to get up close to the roses to inhale their sweet scent, or reach out and touch the long grass or the fluffy pods on the trees, but we don't because we think we might look silly or be judged if others are around.

The more we can sink into our own pleasure and sensuality in small areas of life, the more easily we'll be able to attract in and hold bigger and more significant experiences of pleasure in our lives.

I realised a while back that as a lightworker, it's my job to show up in the world as who I really am and to share my journey with others.

To be the weird girl that bends down to stroke the grass. To be the woman who takes care of her skin (another form of sensuality) and inspires others. To be the one who overshares on Instagram so others know it's OK to show up in their truth too.

I realise that I'm here to share the concept of pleasure in its purest form so that others can let go of shame and judgement and drop into their own sacred sensuality.

Journal Prompts:

- What brings you deep pleasure and joy?
- What do you feel is your most heightened sense?
- What are you not asking for that you really desire in your life?

DISCIPLINE AND DEVOTION

Growing up, I was always the girl (and adult!) who didn't finish things. I'd start art and craft projects and leave them half-finished. I'd buy new hobby supplies and then get bored after using them once or twice, or they'd stay in their box and never get used at all – like the time I thought it would be cool to make soy candles, so bought everything I needed which of course ended up in a charity shop after years gathering dust in the garage!

In my work as a self-employed personal trainer and later as an intuitive copywriter, I'd fill so many notebooks with creative ideas and business plans but never went back to them. All that brilliance just sitting on paper in boxes and drawers around the house.

In all honesty, I still do that, and in many respects this book fell into that category too – sitting on my computer as a document since 2020! It wasn't like I didn't *want* to write the book or bring any of those ideas and plans to life, I simply didn't have the discipline or devotion to make them happen. Or so I thought.

In 2023, after various ADHD-themed posts and videos kept appearing on my Instagram and YouTube feeds, I decided to watch. I resonated instantly! And so, in true ADHD form, I fell down the rabbit hole consuming hours of content over the next few days and talking about it endlessly with my kids!

'Not everything is a symptom of ADHD mum!' was the response I got after a few days. And while that's true, it opened up a whole new perspective on my life and why I am the way I am, particularly when it comes to finishing projects – especially ones that didn't excite me or have an imminent deadline.

Suddenly, little Lorraine who'd carried this huge weight on her shoulders for forty-something years that she *wasn't good enough* or somehow *broken* for not being able to follow through on her ideas and plans – when others seem to do it so effortlessly – understood that she was actually OK. Maybe it wasn't just because she was a 'Gemini who got bored easily', maybe there was another reason?

When I look back over my lifetime, I can see that there are in fact many things that I've committed to for a long time, and that's because they light me up, feel aligned to my values and support my constant desire for growth and expansion. One of those things is healthy eating. Ever since I first figured out ways to cure my headaches and help my bloating and gut issues as a young teenager, I've always deeply trusted my own wisdom in this area and feel my best when I eat intuitively and in a way that aligns to my beliefs.

Learning new skills is another area I've always shown consistent devotion. In my adult life, in addition to retraining in fitness and nutrition in my twenties, I've completed a degree with the Open University, a management diploma, an HR certificate, an adult education tutor certificate, taken numerous online coaching and business courses and spent hours on Duolingo learning Italian, Spanish and a dash of Hebrew and Swedish!

I honestly couldn't imagine life without learning and have always joked that I'll probably take a course in Volcanology when I'm in my eighties!

Weight training is the third thing that's been a constant in my life since first using the school multi-gym in PE when I was fifteen! It's only in the last few years (initially because of the pandemic lockdowns) that I've not been in the gym and it's definitely had a huge impact on my physical and mental health and wellbeing. Now, when I'm back in the gym or training with weights at home on a regular basis it feels sooooo good!

So, what's the difference? Why can I stick to some things for decades and give up on (or forget about) other things within a matter of hours?

For me, I believe it comes down to a lack of self-worth. The stories and limiting beliefs that swirl subconsciously around my mind, stealing my dreams and creating stress in my body.

When you don't believe you're very good at something, it's easiest not to try. Why try and then fail?

And at a deeper level, perhaps the stories we tell ourselves are based on years of cultural programming and our family's experiences.

For example, if no one in your life has ever been 'rich', and all you ever heard growing up was that rich people are 'snobby', 'mean' or 'crooked', then at some level you'll resist becoming (financially) rich for fear of being labelled in the same negative way or judged by your family, friends or community.

Or, if no one in your family has ever been an entrepreneur, business owner or freelancer, the chances are high that your family will be afraid for you to take that path and fill your head with all the reasons why it's not a 'safe and secure' route and 'what if...?'. For some people, this negativity and doubt will lead them to stick to the safe, well-trodden route, while for others it will fuel the desire to step out of the box and prove everyone wrong.

Low self-worth can grow out of many different childhood scenarios and traumas. I'm not a psychology expert or trauma-informed coach, but if you're resonating with this, I highly recommend doing some research and lots of journalling to figure out the core reasons for your current feelings, behaviours and reactions as an adult.

Once I realised that my low self-worth stemmed from always feeling like I didn't fit in, and therefore having to bend my own desires and boundaries to fit in with others and be liked and accepted, it gave me a whole new perspective.

Over the last ten to fifteen years of deep inner work and spiritual growth, I've learnt a lot about myself and my motivations. In order to have good levels of self-discipline, I have to be devoted to my dreams while also staying connected to my intuition. When I'm tapped into my intuition and listening to my soul's desires, I can feel when the everyday goals and to-do lists are aligned with that bigger picture, or not.

Sometimes the things we believed we wanted are no longer a good fit for who we've become.

Or, we realise that we were aiming for specific goals that were based on fear or external validation. Like losing weight to 'fit' a culturally accepted beauty standard. Or aiming for a certain level of financial wealth in order to be seen as successful. Or following the path of job > marriage > house > kids just because it's what our parents and grandparents did, without stopping to ask if that will really make us happy.

If, like me, you've been active in the online business space for a number of years, you will be familiar with the concept of *'stepping into who you want to be'* – or, in other words, acting as the person you dream of becoming before certain things (like money, a partner, a home, kids, the dream job, etc.) are actually a reality in your life.

In my experience, this isn't something you read once and are instantly able to achieve. It takes months or years of slowly chipping away at the external programming and limiting beliefs and putting things into practice bit by bit before you arrive at that lightbulb moment of realisation.

That moment where you actually *feel* it in your cells and *know* it within every fibre of your being.

I had to let go of twenty years of saying *'I really should meditate but I don't have the time and it's too slow for me'* before the penny actually dropped!

After years of dipping in and out of guided meditations and visualisations, I finally committed to meditating every day from 1 January 2021. After the year that was 2020 (!), combined with various triggers within my personal life that got me looking deeper into my own psyche, it felt like the perfect time to devote myself to a daily practice.

In order to keep myself accountable, I set up a spreadsheet where I recorded daily how many minutes I'd meditated for, which YouTube track I used and the time of day. Once I'd reached about twenty-five days, I felt like the new habit was embedded and I no longer needed to track those details.

This method of physical tracking worked well for me because it gave me little dopamine hits every time I saw my achievements snowball.

(This is something I now understand is linked to ADHD as people whose brains are wired this way seek high-dopamine activities and rewards. Which is why breaking down goals into smaller daily activities or micro-activities works so well as the rewards build up and create that feel-good factor that we're more likely to stick to.)

Once I realised that I *was* capable of sticking to an activity long-term, it boosted my self-worth which gave me the momentum to add another activity.

In February 2022, after far too much staying indoors during the pandemic, I decided to start walking every day. The only boundary I set for myself was that it had to be every single day, regardless of the weather or whether I actually wanted to go out. I had no distance, duration or step count goals, just simply to get outside in nature. Again, with the help of a spreadsheet (which I kept for over a year and a half), I tracked my daily walks, location, time and any interesting notes - like exploring a new place, walking with a friend or if I was feeling unwell. I'm so proud of myself for being consistent with a daily walking routine for over two years, walking millions of steps and being ready to take on other fitness challenges.

My increased confidence also led me to say YES to a house and dog-sitting invitation from a friend in Spain, something I probably would have said no to a year or two earlier.

The moral of my story is that you'll never achieve your goals in a healthy, fun and enjoyable way if you're setting them from a place of fear, or needing external validation. Instead, they must come from a place of love, from deep within ourselves; to acknowledge that we are enough, we are worthy, and it's OK to put ourselves first. As many others have written, it's about being *self-ish* – choosing to put your own self first and truly believing that you are worth your own time, love and energy.

YOU GET TO HAVE IT ALL!

As a child, you were probably given choices like butter or jam on your toast, not both.

An ice cream or a slice of cake for dessert, not both.

Crisps or chocolate as a lunchbox treat, not both.

The subliminal message within in those choices was the understanding that it was wrong to have both; that people who ate both were greedy.

Unfortunately, this kind of cultural programming spread much further and deeper than our food choices.

As women, we grew up believing we could have either a career or a family. Not both.

I'd love to say that things have moved on since the 1970s and 80s, but even now, women are still criticised for their choices and carry a deep wound within that eats away at their self-worth and deprives them of having the life they dream of.

Maybe I can't have it all…

Maybe I am being selfish…

Maybe I am wrong for choosing this path…

But I'm here to tell you that you're an adult and you're able to choose whatever you desire for yourself. If you want two desserts, you can eat them! If you want a family and a career and a gorgeous home, you can absolutely have it all. This is your life, and you get to choose exactly how you live it.

Remember…

You *can* have both.

You don't have to choose.

It's not either/or.

You can have all that you desire.

And live a life that feels nourishing, expansive, safe and joyful.

It all starts with gratitude.

A grateful heart for all that you have and all that you are.

Affirmation:

Place your left hand on your heart as you say these affirmations out loud:

I am enough.

I have a pure heart and a kind soul.

I am grateful for all that I have and all that I am.

My life is filled with love, safety and joy.

I am grateful for the abundance of opportunities that appear unexpectedly yet at the perfect moment.

I am rich in so many ways .

My life is an ever-unfolding journey for which I am truly grateful.

Thank you.

I love you.

SLIPPING BACK INTO FEAR

While living and experiencing this magnificent life from a place of love is wonderful, we have to accept that at some points we will always slip back into moments of fear-based reaction or energy. For some it might be for just a nanosecond and instantly noticeable, while for others it will slowly and subtly weave its way back into everyday life, taking longer to notice and become aware of.

It's also important to note that fear is not a negative emotion. You're not a bad or broken person for acting or reacting from a place of fear. Instead, fear should be treated with love and as an invitation to look deeper within.

The inner work, healing and pathway to new levels of personal growth are never complete. There will always be periods of expansion and periods of contraction. Periods of rapid growth and transformation and periods that slow down so much we might wonder if we're moving forward at all.

When we slip into fear-based energy, it's usually accompanied by a physical feeling of energy contracting, gripping us tightly and twisting our stomach into knots or making our neck and shoulder muscles stiffen.

It's not a weakness to slip into fear and react, but it is our responsibility to notice it and course-correct as soon as possible. It might be an apology after saying hurtful words in an argument. Or choosing to unfollow people on social media who make you feel bad about your lifestyle or appearance. Or blocking your ex-partner so you don't make up stories in your head that they've moved on so well while you're still struggling to get back into dating.

And after that swift course-correction, it's important to devote some time to look deeper within to reveal *why* we began acting that way. Usually, the things that trigger us are reflections of our own life, or things that are missing that we deeply crave.

Journal Prompts:

- Can you think of a moment when you slipped into fear-based energy? (Go with the first thing that pops into your head, even if it's not the most recent or seemingly relevant to life right now.)

- How did you feel in that moment? What were the physical sensations you felt in your body?

- Can you recall other moments when you had the same feelings and sensations? What was the cause? Is there a link between them all?

- How do you react in these moments of fear-based energy? Do you pick a fight, withdraw from the conversation, slip into self-loathing or start using food, alcohol, sex, drugs or exercise as a way to numb the feelings?

- How do your reactions make you feel? How do they make others feel? What would you love to change?

- What is the opposite of this fear-based energy for you? How does it look when you're happy, relaxed and feeling an abundance of love in your life?

A PAUSE FOR GRATITUDE

I am so grateful that I chose a less conventional life path and to have met so many amazing people who've embellished my journey with their own unique blend of music and magic.

I am so grateful to be living in an era where there exists so much vocabulary to describe our human existence and the duality of life on planet Earth.

I am so grateful to have been born into a culture, a country and a timeline where freedom of speech and freedom of expression is not only permitted but is encouraged.

And I am beyond grateful to be able to share my thoughts, ideas, experiences and nuggets of wisdom in a book that might just spark transformation in your life, and many others who pick up this book.

It's an honour and a privilege to be here today, as a fifty-year-old woman, healthy, happy and deeply excited for the next chapter of life, love and laughter.

PLANTING THE SEEDS
OF THE FUTURE

I believe that one of the best things we can do for the next generation is to plant trees – and to stop cutting down so many of our beautiful ancient trees and forests, of course.

I've always felt connected to the energy of trees and as a child I loved spending sunny summer days sat in the shade of our large apple tree, reading, drawing or just sitting peacefully watching nature do its wonderful thing. I also loved going on trips to the New Forest in Hampshire where we'd run and walk through the forest, jump over the large roots, swing from branches and sometimes see the famous New Forest ponies.

As a new mother back in the early 2000s, one of my dreams was to own a home with a large garden so I could plant young saplings and watch them grow as my children grew – taking photos each year to track their simultaneous growth. Trees that would still be standing for my grandchildren and beyond.

Unfortunately, buying property wasn't on the cards for me, but I did what I could in our rented accommodation, and love the fact that there's now a huge, mature cherry tree somewhere in Jersey that we initially bought and planted after the passing of one of our guinea pigs – named Cherry!

I've always wanted an orchard for as long as I can remember. I have this romantic notion of picking my own fruit, making jams and sharing my abundant harvest with others. As someone who eats a diet rich in plants, I'd love to create a thriving organic vegetable garden packed with huge kale leaves, broccoli and sweet potatoes and a never-ending supply of parsley and mint in my little kitchen herb garden. My Pinterest vision boards are filled with images of this 'dream' lifestyle that I hope one day soon I'll manifest into reality.

When it comes to planting the seeds for our own future, I feel it's important to remember that we go through the same seasonal cycles as plants and trees. We are cyclical beings (especially women whose bodies go through monthly changes), and it's natural for us to go through periods of summer 'bloom' and quiet, introspective 'wintering'. There are times when we'll grow fast and times when it might feel dark or bleak, but we can always trust that the new shoots of life will appear, just as reliably as spring comes after winter.

Journal Prompts:

- What seeds are you planting now that will bring you joy and abundance in the future?

- How are you tending to your garden of life? Do you nurture your body, your relationships and your career in a way that will bring the best harvest at a later date?

- Which season do you feel you're in right now? Are you at peace with that season or are you always trying to push to be in a different place? (E.g. Constantly hustling and 'blooming' like summer and not taking any time to let go of what no longer serves you (autumn) or taking time to rest and rejuvenate (winter).)

QUANTUM SHIFTS

What if we are living multiple timelines in any given moment?

This concept fascinates me and often leads me deep into internet rabbit holes where I can be lost for minutes or hours and receive many aha moments and realisations. Moments where the dots connect and patterns form.

Go back to the question above and take a few moments to ponder this concept. Feel free to jot down the thoughts and feelings that pop into your mind before you read on…

Here are some of the things I've learnt about quantum energetic shifts:

(Quantum shifts are defined in the personal growth space as radical shifts in mindset that energetically bring about an elevated quality of life; bringing you closer to living in alignment with your personal desires, dreams and goals.)

- All the while we're stuck in the past, we can't quantum leap.

- In order to move forward, you have to let go of the past; of old beliefs, habits and patterns of being.

- You can't quantum leap from your 'head'.

- If you're always thinking about failure or being stuck, then that's what you'll get! *(Watch your language!)*

- Quantum leaps don't make sense; they're not logical to the human mind.

- It's never about the 'how'. It's an energy thing! Release the logical, human way of doing things.

- Keep creating space for amazing things to come into your life. Let go of clutter, old energy, limiting beliefs, people and places that no longer feel like a match for your vibration.

- Practice gratitude daily. This is the most potent way to keep your energy at a high vibration.

- *How* and *when* do not matter when it comes to quantum shifting. Anything is possible!

- Resistance slows everything down. Let go. Breathe. Move on.

The practice of visualisation – whether in a meditative state or through the art of creating a vision board – helps us to picture what we want and tap into how that might *feel*.

But creating our 'dream life' doesn't just happen by magic! It's a combination of visualisation + letting go + gratitude + setting intentions + daily choices (taking action).

The energetics behind everything we do are just as important (if not more so) than the actions we take. For example, it's commonly known that many celebrities or lottery winners who suddenly receive huge amounts of money end up broke or bankrupt because they've never cleared up the negative energy they carry around wealth and money.

Here's a simple way to shift the energetics in your life to allow an abundance of opportunities, money and love into your world:

- Practice daily gratitude – through journalling and in your daily interactions with nature and people.

- Use visualisations and vision boards to bring to life your true desires. Make sure to leave visual cues all around your environment that you'll see daily – e.g. your phone lock screen, the front cover of your journal, your laptop background, a note in your wallet.

- Use journalling and the energy of the full moons to continuously let go of old energy and limiting beliefs.

- Set intentions (rather than goals) that are based on how you want to feel (rather than what you want to do). Set intentions of different sizes for the year, the month, the week and each day.

- Aim to ensure that your daily actions match your intentions. For example, if you want to be fit enough to hike Kilimanjaro with friends next year, you'll want to practice hiking regularly on uneven ground with a backpack. If that's not possible, you might want to join a gym, get personal training sessions tailored to hiking at altitude and walk to work instead of taking the car.

Journal Prompts:

- What has been my biggest struggle?
- What patterns do I keep repeating?
- What do I *really* want? And is that actually *my* dream or just the thing I think I *should* want?
- What am I willing to give up to achieve my dream?
- How can I practice living with gratitude?

'You can love a caged bird
so much you clip her wings
and declare freedom.
While denying the very
thing that makes her free.

If you truly love the caged
bird, open the cage
and let her fly.'

– MICHAEL T. COE

JOY

What does joy look like to you? How does it feel?

Is it feeling the heat on your skin when you step off the plane in a foreign country? Or the tingle of excitement as you're making love for the first time with someone new? Or the mouth-watering anticipation of that first bite of a decadent chocolate dessert?

As amazing as all these experiences are, finding joy in the simple things in our everyday life is, I believe, a huge part of living a happy life.

It always makes me smile watching my rabbits eagerly snatch kale leaves from me in the mornings, chomping the leaves as their little noses twitch. Or the way my cat curls up on a cushion on my lap every evening, hanging his chin over the edge and purring deeply as I stroke his silky fur.

Joy and gratitude are deeply entwined: feeling joy and being thankful for all the moments of magic in the mundane is a fulfilling way to live.

Notes from My Journal (while housesitting in Spain):

> I just had a thought while hanging out the washing: I am living a beautiful life because it's filled with tiny micro-moments of beauty and magic. Like just now, hanging up the freshly washed sheets on the terrace, looking up at the pure blue sky. How lucky am I to have lived this life filled with such beautiful moments of wonder and awe. I have everything I need. Anything else is just a bonus! THIS is real life. Not the hustle of a business or the pursuit of money; but just here and now, the present moment, simply doing all the small things that bring me joy. I am so lucky, so blessed, so happy.

It's important to note that we don't have to be in the pursuit of joy and happiness 24/7. In fact, actively *trying* to be happy is probably likely to create resistance that only holds you back from a peaceful, joy-filled existence.

Nobody is perfect. We all have to constantly tune into what's most important to us and allow ourselves the space and perspective to decide whether the things we're choosing are of high value or low value to us. Asking: is this supporting my goals and dreams, or going against them?

This is what living in alignment is all about.

On the occasions when we're about to choose something of low value, it's important to reflect, ponder and expand on that to understand why we are driven to make that choice. Ask yourself: Am I tired? Frustrated? Exhausted? Hungry? Bored? What could I do instead to honour or nourish myself?

When you start to feel like you're stuck in a low vibration energetically, sit with it and feel into it. Where is it in your body? What emotions is it bringing up?

Realise that you have two main choices: allow the darkness to take over, continue to spiral, scroll social media on your phone or do other low-vibe activities that effectively waste your time.

Or, step into the light. Take an active break or hang out with a high-vibe person or bunch of people. Do something entirely unrelated to work or whatever was causing the issues – have fun and be present.

By regularly practicing to actively live in a state of joy and gratitude while simultaneously checking in with your feelings and clearing energetic blocks will help you to live a full, wild life, free from convention and always fulfilled and joyful.

Journal Prompts:

- Make a list of 100 things that bring you joy.

A hundred might sound like a lot, but as you get into the flow of opening your heart and feeling joy, you'll be amazed at the words that spill onto the page.

STAY CURIOUS

Recipe for a happy life: stay curious.

I honestly couldn't imagine life without an endless quest for learning! Of course, this does mean I'm frequently distracted by random thoughts that take me off on a winding journey deep inside the world wide web, but I've always felt that these little 'curiosity trails', as I like to call them, are part of a bigger web of connections that make us who we are.

If I've randomly read or heard a piece of information, I can guarantee that somewhere in the minutes, hours or days that follow I will use that stored information in a conversation (or in my writing) that forms new connections in the invisible energetic web that connects us all.

To me, curiosity, conversations, listening and learning are all intricately entwined. It's how we thrive best as humans. After all, we are social creatures that benefit from love, connection and a sense of community.

Having a curious mind is both a natural trait and a learned skill. It comes very naturally to us as children. If you're a parent you might feel exhausted with all the 'why?', questions, but this is a vital part of the growing process and leads to more curious, creative adults.

Being curious as an adult is important to society and evolution because it sparks learning and leads to exchanges of ideas and creative conversations that drive forward innovation and growth.

As humans, we have an innate desire to learn, grow and seek out new experiences, but if we're feeling stuck, stressed out by the burden of life's challenges, or going through health issues or disease, it's normal that our curiosity and desire to learn might be dampened.

Fear plays a big part in this. If we're afraid of failure, we're unlikely to start learning a new skill, switch jobs or leave a bad relationship.

Reignite your curious nature with a dose of love...

If fear has squashed your curiosity, you can reclaim it by dropping into a loving energy. Start with meditation and a little gratitude journalling (which generally helps in almost every occasion when we feel a bit 'off').

Devote some time to sitting in peace and stillness, or walking in nature, to create space in your mind for curiosity to bloom.

Ask yourself, what would I really *love* to learn? What skill would I love to develop or strengthen?

Notice if fear-based energy pops up almost immediately in the form of limiting beliefs around money *(taking up that hobby or enrolling on that course would be really expensive)*, self-worth *(I could never do that, I'll never be any good at that)*, or time/energy *(I don't have time to fit that in, I'd never have the energy to work, study and look after my family)*.

Remember that if something is really important to you, you'll always find a way to make it happen.

We don't like to admit it, but most of us are guilty of prioritising things that aren't really important to us simply because we're tired, stressed, hungry, sad or bored. Like binge-watching Netflix, ordering food on Uber Eats or scrolling TikTok in bed til late.

We need to get curious about our inner world before we can truly indulge curiosity on a bigger scale.

Before we invest huge sums of money into training or commit to a year-long certification course, we've got to look inward at our own limiting beliefs, patterns and behaviours.

This self-reflection will help us to see why we sabotage our own dreams and goals.

Why we're afraid to learn to play guitar because we don't believe we'll ever be good enough so why bother! Why we've never immersed ourselves in learning astrology because we think that others will judge us for being 'woo-woo'. Why we've never booked that singles group adventure holiday because we're scared of failing or looking stupid in front of others.

Getting curious about your inner world will support you in getting curious about the bigger and more meaningful things in your life.

Journal Prompts:

- Can you remember the last time you got lost in your own version of a 'curiosity trail'? How did it feel? Did it give you a sense of satisfaction and leave you yearning for more?

- What would your inner child really love to do? How do they want to bring more playfulness, curiosity and joy to your life as an adult?

- What would you love to do even if you knew you might fail?

TURNING FIFTY

I never knew that turning fifty would be such a huge turning point in my life; a period of unparalleled transformation and growth.

Turning forty was fun. Inside I felt like I was still only twenty-something and just getting started in life. I was fit, strong and healthy and felt empowered and invincible. I'd envisioned my forties to be fabulous! A continuation of my energetic, lively, passion-filled thirties. But, that wasn't to be the case.

Looking back, my forties were a decade filled with big life changes, health issues, financial struggles and almost completely devoid of romantic love. But hey, without life's challenges, we wouldn't grow, evolve and become the amazing human beings we are today!

From forty-seven onwards, I could feel the energy slowly shifting to something deeper and more potent. My heart could feel that the next chapter of my life would be a powerful one and I knew deep in the depths of my soul that everything would work out in the best possible way.

'If not this then something better.'

With the astrological sign of Sagittarius ruling my moon and my ascendant (my rising sign), I was born to be a traveller and lover of freedom and wild adventures. In my teens and twenties, I travelled a lot, taking numerous holidays in the Greek Islands and later exploring California multiple times between 1999 and 2002, as well as starting a new life in Jersey in the late 1990s.

In 2022, after the pandemic, a beautiful soul sister who splits her time between the UK and Spain offered me the chance to house-sit and look after her gorgeous dog – a fluffy Cockapoo with boundless energy – for six weeks during the depths of the British winter. Of course I said yes!

I'm actually quite afraid of some types of dogs and will actively avoid them when they're off the lead on the beaches, and I've been known to turn around on narrow cliff paths if I see loose dogs heading in my direction! However, I do love fluffy, sweet-natured dogs – like Cockapoos, Labradoodles and Golden Retrievers, so I knew that in looking after my friend's dog I'd not only have a lot of fun but would also be taking steps outside my comfort zone and releasing some of the fear-based energy in my body.

And so, in January 2023, a few months before turning fifty, I boarded a flight to Gibraltar, feeling excited to see the sunshine but knowing that this was also going to be a huge period of growth and transformation. *(In fact, I'd planned to finish writing this book there…it didn't happen!)*

I had an absolutely brilliant time walking my friend's dog for miles each day and we spent every night snuggled together in bed! *(Well, he took up most of it, as dogs generally do!)*

At a time of year when Britain is enveloped in a never-ending cycle of wind, rain and grey cloudy days, being in Southern Spain was an absolute blessing. It allowed me to be immersed in nature every day, watching the tiny wrens in the hedge around the garden, looking up to watch the noisy parakeets flying from palm tree to palm tree, and immersing myself in the peaceful sight of sea birds on the estuary at sunset, with the rock of Gibraltar in the distance. Bliss!

While I was in Spain, I felt a deep gratitude for my life and the opportunities I'd created simply by showing up in my truth and building beautiful connections and friendships. And it was from this space of love and gratitude that I was offered another house sit at the end of year, by a friend who lives in Australia!

Coincidentally, Sydney had also been on my daughter's vision board for 2023, so we jumped at the chance to go for a month over Christmas and look after my friend's gorgeous cat.

Arriving in Sydney in December was amazing. I was blown away by the city and instantly fell in love with its energy as a vibrant, multi-cultural city that sparkles at night and glows in sunshine all day. I honestly feel that if I'd gone there in my twenties I would never have left!

As my daughter had already decided she wanted to stay on in Sydney after our trip together, I was not only seeing the place for the first time through my eyes, but also through the lens of my daughter's future home (at least for a year or two); a place I might be lucky enough to come back to again and again.

The Blue Mountains just outside of Sydney were magical on a whole other level. This ancient forest spreads for miles, as far as the eyes can see, casting a distinctive blue hue and fading into paler tones across the ridges into the distance.

I already knew I wanted a similar image of pastel hues and mountain ridges for the front cover of *Raising Wild Birds*, so seeing this in real life (the photos don't do it justice) was an absolute treat that filled me with so much joy and made me feel pretty emotional.

Saying YES to these two travel opportunities in the year I turned fifty is no coincidence! The Universe lined them up beautifully for me because it knew I had put in the work and was ready for a huge shift.

Turning fifty can be a challenging time for a woman because she's probably hovering on the edge of menopause and might be on the brink of a new chapter where her children become adults and move away from home. For some women this can be a difficult time, feeling a loss of purpose, invisible and sad. If that's you, I hope that this book has ignited a spark within you to seek out new adventures and start living life in a way that lights your heart and fuels your inner fire.

For me, fifty is like a midway point with so much more left to see and do. I've always been able to see myself as an old woman and often visualise myself at my 100th birthday celebrations! In fact, I used to think that one day when I'm really old, grey and wrinkled, my physical body will finally match the old soul that's always been inside me. I've always felt like the 'wise woman of the village' that people would come to for guidance or healing and struggled with believing that people would take me seriously. *(They did of course, but I had to learn to work through those limiting beliefs and learn to love and value myself and see my worth.)*

As I approach fifty-one, I'm excited and honoured that I'll at last be holding a physical printed copy of *Raising Wild Birds* and will be able to proudly see it on the shelves in bookstores. Where it goes after that, who knows? I trust that it will fall into the hands of the people who need it most; those – just like you – who are ready for the inevitable shifts and transformation in their lives.

Journal Prompts:

- Are you approaching a 'big' birthday? How do you feel about it? Reflect on the last decade and summarise it in a few paragraphs or bullet points.

- What are you most excited about for the decade ahead? Do you already feel intuitively that things are about to change? That you are on the cusp of something magical?

- If you're in your late thirties or early forties, how do you feel about perimenopause and menopause? Are you afraid, apprehensive, resigned to the fact that your body or health will change?

LOVE AT FIRST SIGHT

Flying into Queenstown, New Zealand, after our month in Sydney, cracked my heart open. There's something about flying over snowcapped mountains that ignites deep emotion within me. It's as if I'm a bird with huge wings, like an eagle or condor, soaring elegantly; peaceful and serene.

As we descended into the airport, the size of the mountains was evident, making our plane look small and insignificant (it definitely wasn't!). My first impression of Queenstown Airport was how small and friendly it was, especially coming from a big city like Sydney (which is friendly too, but not in the same way as a smaller town).

I fell in love with New Zealand from the very start, but in a different way to Sydney. Sydney brought me back to life; made me feel like a twenty-five-year-old again and reignited my zest for life and adventure.

New Zealand on the other hand connected with me on a deeper level, like a remembering of times gone by, thousands of years ago. It was as if I knew the land already, its energy and undulations.

Perhaps it's a past-life thing, or simply the energy of Mother Nature, Gaia, herself that courses through all our veins. We are of the Earth, an endless cycle. We are born of the Earth and after we die, we become the Earth – the sea, the plants, the animals, the sky… The continuous cycle of nature. Both harsh and gentle, ugly and beautiful,

While Sydney challenged me with its heat and humidity, Queenstown challenged my lungs and leg muscles as we hiked up hills and trails in the quest for those unbeatable panoramic views of mountains and lakes.

The scenery in New Zealand's South Island is breathtaking. Crystal-clear lakes. Mountains with jagged snow-capped peaks. Vivid turquoise glacier lakes. Pink and purple lupins dotted across the landscape. Mountain ranges in pastel blues, getting lighter and lighter into the distance.

Without the housesitting opportunity in Australia, we would never have 'hopped over' to New Zealand and I would not have experienced such beauty and love during the year I turned fifty. I know in my heart and soul that this trip was divinely led and divinely timed to enable me to step into the next level of my life.

Thank you, Universe.

THUNDERING WATERFALLS

Ever since I returned from my travels, I've been gushing about my experiences to anyone who'll listen!

As I write these final chapters of my book, I'm feeling deeply emotional, grateful and connected to my inner 'wild woman' who craves adventure, travel and new experiences.

My creativity is potent, flowing out of me as fast as the incredible waterfalls we witnessed in New Zealand, and crashing onto the page – whether that's in this book, in my client work or on one of the many social media platforms or blogs I write on each week.

Just as there's so much more I would love to see and do in Australia and New Zealand, I know that there's so much more I want to do using my innate gift for writing to share experiences, knowledge and wisdom.

In my journal, I wrote:

> Is travel escapism? Is it running away? Running from
> fears or responsibilities? Or are we running towards
> our destiny? What if I was always meant to be there?

What do you think? How do you feel about travel?

Are there parts of your life you're running away from?
What could you run towards instead?

SOARING HIGH

As I write the ending to this book, I can feel intuitively that everything is falling into place.

I can see how I needed to get to this point in my life in order to be able to complete the 'story' of *Raising Wild Birds*. To know deep in my heart and soul that I'm on the cusp of 'soaring high'; stepping into my magnificence as a menopausal woman with a whole fifty years or more ahead of her.

I finally feel as if I've grown into the woman I was always destined to be.

And do you know what's even better?

I *don't* have life all figured out! I don't have any of the things I was attached to having (because society told me I 'should'!) – like a mortgage, a husband, a curated wardrobe or a 'perfect' body!

What I do have is infinitely better...

I have an inner peace that allows me to make decisions and take action from a place of calm and love.

I have resilience and inner strength. I've faced some fears, overcome challenges and looked deep within at my shadow side and come out the other side stronger and more in love with who I am. And I know that my resilience will always keep me moving forward, even in difficult times.

I have curiosity, dreams and a growth mindset – and with those, life will keep continuing to expand and evolve, opening up new opportunities and possibilities beyond my wildest imagination.

I have beautiful connections with incredible soul sisters and heart-centred entrepreneurs around the world, and closer to home, whose conversations and connections I deeply appreciate.

I have two incredible grown-up daughters who are finding their own way in the world, following their hearts and bringing their vision boards to life. And together we're forging beautiful new deeper relationships as adults.

Letting them unfurl their wings and fly is the most beautiful gift I can give them, and myself.

Journal Prompts:

- What do you have in your life that you value so much more than the 'things' society expects us to have?

- Do you feel like you've grown into the person you were always destined to be? If not, how might that look and feel?

LETTING GO

It's no surprise to me that I'm writing this chapter on a full moon – a magical moment of synchronicity as I let go of this book to my publishing team and simultaneously release the negative energy and guilt I've held onto for the last two years that this book 'should' be finished!

Writing and publishing *Raising Wild Birds* is like the bookmark between chapters of my life. It marks the ending of my life until age fifty, and the beginning of my new life after – including life as a published author. *(I'm not-so-secretly curious about the opportunities that might bring!)*

I can now see how my trip to Australia and New Zealand was a powerful catalyst in reconnecting with the energy of my book and committing to getting it finished. Although I didn't actually write while I was away, simply being in the energy of expansion, adventure and exploration was enough to quantum leap to new levels.

Never underestimate the power of a change of location.

In Australia, the heat and humidity were pretty intense and there were numerous times I complained about my dripping wet, beetroot-coloured face and the sweat running down my back – especially if that was before I'd even got dressed or put any make-up on! And we won't even mention trying to get a tight sports bra on or off in those conditions…

But, getting hot and sweaty every day on walks around the city or on beachfront trails felt amazing for my body. It was like my skin was clearing out the toxins of the last few years of stress – physical and energetic toxins, blocks and stagnant energy sweated out and washed away in the shower.

Moving my body and sweating daily sped up the flow of energy within me faster than any therapy session could ever have done. My mind cleared and I felt happier than I had done in years. It was as if I was in the perfect place at the perfect time. Which of course we always are!

If you're feeling stuck, overwhelmed or stressed, move your body in a way that elevates your heart rate and makes you sweat.

Of course, planet Earth is a planet of polarity, so we only experience joy, happiness and flow because we also experience pain, sadness and feeling 'stuck'.

Returning home in the middle of winter to an endless stream of grey, wet and windy days became a struggle after the initial high of my holiday wore off.

I went from feeling creative, extroverted, excited to see people and in flow with my creativity to a sudden wall of darkness. I had no desire to do anything remotely productive, even though my busy mind kept reminding me there was so much I wanted and needed to do. For a few days, I slipped into a spiral of low energy, scrolling social media, binge-watching Netflix, going to bed too late and not setting foot outside for over twenty-four hours!

Thankfully, after the last new moon passed, my energy and enthusiasm returned. I started being proactive, seeking new opportunities and strengthening relationships.

This is a great example of the power of transformational inner work and long-term commitment to personal growth and expansion. The more work we've put in, the faster we're able to get back on track after something derails us.

Just like having a healthy, flexible, youthful body in our seventies and eighties is a result of all the times we exercised, ate healthy and got enough rest in our younger years, instead of taking the easy, more comfortable option.

Choosing to spend a few minutes a day keeping a gratitude journal, drinking water, cooking food from scratch and walking in nature might not feel like it's doing a tremendous amount today, but when you do that every day for a month, a year, a decade or more, the shift will be enormous.

Journal Prompts:

- What small positive habits have you been doing for a long time already and how have they benefitted you?

- What other habits would you like to add to your daily routine? *(Top tip: Add habits one by one and stack them with existing habits to create long-term change.)*

- Can you think of a time in recent months where you felt like you were in a negative energy slump? How did it feel? What did your habits look like and how quickly did you pick yourself up? What might you do differently next time?

- Can you think of a time in recent months where you felt super creative, in flow, firing on all cylinders and with enough energy for work, family, hobbies and socialising? How did it feel? What were you doing in your life on a regular basis to support your mental and physical wellbeing?

(Pinpointing these things will help build awareness and allow you to strengthen your resilience and adaptability to change.)

- What old habits and limiting beliefs are you choosing to let go of?
- What physical items can you release from your life?

(Letting go and releasing physical clutter and emotional baggage supports the flow of abundance.)

DEATH AND REBIRTH

With every ending comes a new beginning.

We have to let go of old versions of ourselves in order to move forward and embrace who we've become.

Turning fifty and heading towards menopause has meant letting go of the youthful, twenty-nine-year-old version of me I clung onto for so long.

I used to look at old photos, recalling my body size, weight and measurements and wishing I still looked like younger Lorraine. But in staying so attached to who I once was, I never got to know the woman I was becoming in each moment. I was never giving myself a chance to love and appreciate my incredible ageing body in the present moment. I was stuck in the past – and that doesn't help anyone!

So, turning fifty has brought with it a new energy of being reborn. I realise how lucky I am to not only be alive at fifty, but to be healthy, happy and able to make a living through my writing. Ten-year-old Lorraine would be very happy to hear that! (And the fact that I still have pet bunnies to play with every day!)

In 2011, before I'd discovered the power of oracle cards for self-growth and personal insights, I had a tarot reading done by an amazing friend and psychic who's sadly now passed on. I vividly remember the 'death' card coming up which filled me with fear. I didn't realise that death in the tarot signifies rebirth; an ending and a new beginning.

For me, today, that new chapter looks like finding my way as a mother whose children have flown the nest to start their own lives as adults.

Raising confident, happy, kind young people who aren't afraid to follow their dreams is an important part of parenting. After all, just as we miss out on life in the present moment if we cling to the past, so too will we miss out on the next chapter of seeing our children thrive as adults if we cling onto the parent-child dynamic, forever trying to keep them safe and protected from the world.

In the natural world, bird parents can only do so much to raise their chicks. After that, it has to take those first precarious steps along the branch before it can spread its wings and learn to fly. It has to take a risk and figure it out, again and again, just as its parents and grandparents did before it.

The young bird, now almost fully grown, must fly away and fend for itself, until one day, it too will be an adult, soaring high above the treetops or amongst the mountains, inspiring the next generation to spread their wings and reach new heights.

THE END

ACKNOWLEDGMENTS

My beautiful daughters, Nadège and Ayiana. I love and appreciate you so, so much. Your love and support for me and my writing is incredibly special to me and I can't wait to share the next chapter of life with you. I'm so proud of you both. Keep flying high!

Mum. Thank you for loving me in your own beautiful way for the last fifty years. I really appreciate all the support you've given me, especially during the difficult times. Thank you for passing on your love of words and creativity to me and your granddaughters.

Max. Thank you for all your support and encouragement over the last twenty-six years. I'm so grateful for all you do for me and our amazing daughters.

Lins, my guardian angel. Thank you for showing me how to get out of my head and into my heart, even if I wasn't ready back then! Thank you for all the signs you send from the other side, your loving presence will never be forgotten.

Nicola Humber, my writing coach and free-spirited inspiration at The Unbound Writers Mastermind and The Unbound Press. Without your high-vibe sisterhood, unbound writing sessions and silver circle of light, I'd never have got started on this beautiful journey. Thank you for your continued love and support.

Sandy Cousens – Artist and author. Thank you for all your love, support, channelled wisdom and inspiration over the past few years as we navigated shifts in our work and stepped up to write and create our books. I'm so excited to see yours in print soon too!

Natalie Farrell – Cosmic songbird, lightworker and singer. Thank you for being such a beautiful kind, generous and gentle soul whose light shines so brightly through all you do. And for giving me the opportunity to step out of my comfort zone and look after your fur baby Rocket.

Pearl Jordan – Performance and wellbeing specialist, coach and speaker. Thank you for being the best account-ability buddy, friend and inspiration over the last few years. Your words of wisdom always activate me to step into my potential. Thank you for being you and I can't wait to read your book later this year.

Tara Jackson – Author and founder of Empathpreneurs. Your gentle soul, calm creativity and grounded energy is an absolute gift to the world. You inspire me to always be a better version of myself and I love our Zoom catch-ups across the world. Hopefully, one day soon I'll fly to Africa and visit you and experience first-hand the life-changing magic of an incredible continent.

The Unbound Writing Mastermind group – Each and every one of you was hugely inspirational on our monthly calls and I'm so proud of you all for finishing and publishing your books, or for taking the first steps to even begin this rollercoaster of a journey!

Leah Kent – Book coach at Wild Embodied Writing. Thank you for being such a beautiful soul who shares her wisdom so generously. Your words of encouragement really helped me at the halfway point and have stayed with me ever since.

Georgia Varjas – Book writing coach and author. Thank you for your words of encouragement, expert knowledge, brilliant sense of humour and friendship over the last few years. I appreciate all you do and the value you bring to the book-writing community.

Brittney Carmichael – Founder of Shine School, The Elevated Life Club and trailblazing lightworker. Thank you for your friendship, love and sparkle magic over the last nine years and for being the first to inspire me to connect deeper with my inner wisdom through oracle cards and to step into my greatness.

Thank you to my local and international circle of entrepreneurial friends and soul sisters who have been beside me every step of the way and encouraged and supported my book-writing journey.

Thank you to everyone in my Sunday Love Letter circle who indulges my writing, thoughts and ideas on a weekly basis. It really means so much to me that you subscribed and show up each week to read my love letters and to take the time to reply.

Thank you to my friends, family and connections on social media for your beautiful comments, support and love for my writing and unique perspective on life.

ABOUT THE AUTHOR

Lorraine uses her innate gifts as an intuitive writer, lightworker and storyteller in various ways across multiple platforms to ignite curiosity, spark change and activate ripple effects of quiet transformation across the world.

With decades of experience in fitness, nutrition and food coaching, and the last seven years as a professional copywriter for personal brands and heart-centred businesses, Lorraine possesses a unique combination of skills, tools and experiences that gently inspire and motivate others to step into their potential, overcome their fear-based blocks and shine brilliantly.

For more information about working directly
with Lorraine, you can visit her website
www.thesoulfulword.com
or connect across social media
@thesoulfulword and **@raisingwildbirds.love**

Printed in Great Britain
by Amazon

58882878R00162

It's Not about Me

by

Chris Fife

© 9/4/2017

Table of Contents

Introduction

I was sitting in a faculty meeting before the school year started. It was boring as school meetings go. They were repeating the same things as they had the school year before. As I sat there looking at the twelve new teachers at the school, I felt sorry for them and thought about the struggle they would have throughout the year.

I was also getting nervous about the new school year and thought about the terrible classes I had the previous year and all of the returning students I would have as 9th graders. I hoped they matured a little and the school year would go okay.

My thoughts and even some of the words that came out of my mouth to a teacher I sat next to were condescending and negative about the meeting and upcoming school year. I did not feel very excited about the prospect of teaching crazy teenagers again and not having the support of administration and the district in disciplining children.

Then it occurred to me that it was not about me. I had been thinking about this idea for some time in my classroom and in my life in general. The meetings suddenly were not about me. They were about preparing the new teachers for the school year, about getting ready to help all of the returning students, and most of all about the effort of those who prepared the meetings. I suddenly realized that I was being very selfish and needed to change my attitude and the way I was thinking. So I continued to think about that it was not about me, and to my surprise I felt ten times better and the meetings turned out to be better. I also gained a better attitude about the school and about the upcoming school year. My negativity and nervous junk in my mind was gone.

I still have a long way to go for this to sink in. It will take a lot of effort on my part, and I will have a lot of times when I fall into old habits and resist being positive. I want very much to be liberated from my negative thoughts and attitude and to be focused on others. I feel this is an important step in finding the peace and comfort in my life and being able to connect with others to develop a deeper relation with those I care about.

Chapter One: Pride

In my youth I was sad most of the time. I was chronically depressed, had a lot of anxiety, fear, and worried a lot. At the time I simply blamed my situation. I had a low self-esteem and continued to think that I was short, ugly, fat, un-athletic, and a poor communicator. None of this was true except for being short of corse. There are just some things we do not have control over in our lives.

The thing I did have control over were my thoughts, my attitude, and the choices I made. My thoughts and attitude were negative and obsessed with fantasies of being a professional football player, a professional body builder, and a famous actor and singer. I did not make too many choices back then. I generally would just sit home and watch television. Later I did choose to play sports and exercise. But I did not make the choice to practice a musical instrument, or do anything else to work towards the dreams I thought that would magically come.

At the time I was just depressed and somehow thought that when I turned twenty everything would magically happen. I would get married, start a family, get into a high paying career, and be rich and famous. None of this turned out the way I thought it would. Every failure I experienced turned into a tragedy and more depression and negative thoughts. I ended up just floating through school and getting by.

It wasn't until I was an adult and started to learn about how life works that I discovered the flaws in my thinking when I was a kid. I was very selfish and prideful as a kid being consumed with just myself and how miserable my life was. I was either thinking about how bad life was or how I would later on in my life become rich and famous. Sure from time to time I thought of friends, girls, and my family, girls especially. But even when I thought about others it was in my terms of what they would bring in my life. I wanted to have a girl friend to love me. I wanted my parents to give me support and presents. I wanted my friends to be able to play with me.

There were times when in my church I did think about others the way I should have. There were a few times when I acted out of kindness, respect, and compassion to others. It was these times that rooted me in being able to have hope, faith, and love. If it wasn't for this simple lesson of kindness, I would have totally self-destructed. Yet I did not fully grasp this and become more self centered than I should have and ended up paying the price of being depressed and anxious all of the time.

I know now that if I would have thought about doing my best in school for my parents and making them feel good about my accomplishments I would have tried harder in school. If I would have thought about my sisters more, I would have developed a closer relationships with them and would not feel as timid as I do today. I would have not have made the mistakes I had made if I would have thought of my family first. I would have tried harder to have been more successful if I would have thought about how it would have helped my family.

My actions and choices would have been a lot different if I would have thought about my future family and how those decisions would have impacted them. The depression and anxiety would have gone away if I had only thought about others at the time, instead of thinking only of how things effected me. I would have been better in school just by thinking about my teachers and their sacrifice in teaching me.

I definitely would have tried harder with my assignments and studies harder for tests taking them more seriously than I had done if I would have thought about the teachers and how they would have felt by my performance.

Bullied

My childhood was probably a typical middle class American childhood, except that I was bullied relentlessly in elementary school. This of course scared me to the point that I turned inward and did not trust anyone. If I would have thought about it with the perspective of those bullying me, I would have understood things differently.

As a teacher I see many children bullying other children. There are many reasons for this. They may want attention from their peers or even from adults around them. They may be going through tough times and want to take it out on other kids. They may just want to belong to a group which likes to bully other students. It could also be that they think that what they are doing is funny.

What I have realized that is that it was not about me. There was nothing wrong with me when I got bullied. It was about the bully trying to fit in or feel better about himself and those who joined in on the bullying thought that it was either funny or just want to belong to the group.

I also grew up at a time when bullying was not something that was mentioned or even prevented as much in schools. There was a lot of bullying that was accepted by children and adults as a part of life. It seemed like everyone did it at one point in their life. When I was the bully I turned inward and the act was about me having power over the person I was bullying. It was not a good place for me to be, especially since I knew what it was like to be bullied.

My Dad

Part of my depression was what happened when I was at home. My father worked hard to support his family. He taught me to have integrity and to help others. He did have his faults. My dad did use profanity once in a while and that profanity was sometimes used as an insult to me and my sisters. At the time I was scared of my father and thought that he hated me. I could not do anything good enough for him and he did not understand me.

There were a couple of occasions my father would even punish me physically. This made my life at home uneasy. I felt much alone despite having two parents and three sisters. I felt like no one understood me and cared for me. It was really hard for me to connect with my family.

I did not know the whole story about my father. I did not know that he had been married before and went through an ugly divorce. I knew I had some step brothers, but they didn't really live with us. I also didn't know that my dad was struggling to get a good job and finish college. He was under a lot of stress and pressure to raise his family.

I did not know his past either. He grew up in a home where his father was never around and his mother was a little eccentric. He was the oldest of three boys so he had to do a lot around the house. He grew up during the depression and World War II. My father managed to graduate from high school. Started working when he was a teenager and got married young. He had three sons with his first marriage. He also spent a couple years in the military.

My father did all he could just to remain sane. He basically did the best he could under the circumstances. Sure he could have been a little more loving and could have controlled his language. He could have been more mindful of his children's needs and desires. But it wasn't about me. My father loved me and his children. Many of the terrible things he said about me he didn't mean and only said while he was under a lot of stress.

I also didn't know that one time he had received a head injury where he was acting strange. He would get in the back seat of the car and wait there until my mom came and found him and asked him what he was doing. He said, "I'm going to work." He also had some seizures from the injury. He went to the doctor and they gave him some medication that seemed to help him get better. Part of the head injury could have altered his behavior for a while.

My sisters on the other hand learned what was going on with my dad. They understood many of the things I didn't. I didn't know of them having it as hard as I did when I was growing up. So if I would have just thought about what my dad was going through I would have done a lot better.

Dating

I remember wanting to have a girl friend in high school, but no girl seemed to like me. I did go on a couple of dates, but no second dates. Again I was thinking of myself and felt that I was a loser. It was this self-centered attitude that made it difficult for girls to like me. In fact there were a couple of girls that did like me, but I pushed them away by acting nervous around them.

I did the same thing as an adult. I had a lot of first dates, but no second dates. It wasn't until I decided to stop worrying about me and think about my dates for a change. I thought that if I became the best I could and when I did go out on dates I would not worry about a second date and just have fun. I started to show more interest in my dates and what they liked.

A wonderful thing happened when I changed the way I thought about dating. I not only had more fun, I was able to find a wonderful person to marry. Since then I try to think more of her than myself. The more I do this the closer we become.

School and Career

I struggled at school when I was younger and got average grades. In college I started to do better with my grades and since then have excelled with classes I have taken. I found out a secret about school. It is not about me as a student, it is all about the teacher. I found that once I understood what the teacher wanted I just did that and was fine. There were some teachers who expected me to read all of the assigned reading, but did not place too much emphasis on the lectures. Then there were the teachers who did not expect much in the reading and placed more emphasis on the lectures. Most teachers did a little of both. I just learned what the teacher expected and then did it and was able to do great in my classes.

The same lesson I learned in school, I have been able to learn in my career. I went through five years of interview, applications, and prayers trying to get into the teaching profession. I went to interview with myself in mind. It is important to be able to show your best self in an interview. Yet when you go to an interview being nervous and worried about getting the job chances are you will not get the job.

I was a nervous wreck in my interview. I came with the attitude that I was a loser and they probably would not hire me. I had some good interview and did really well, but then did not get hired, so it reinforced my self defeating thoughts.

I realized again it was not about me. There were dozens of other people interviewing for the jobs I had interviewed for. Many of the people probably needed the job more than I did, and some of them were probably more qualified than I was. Also the principals doing the interview had there own idea of who they wanted to hire and I did not fit their profile. In hindsight the principals that did not hire me were doing me a favor. I was not right for some of the jobs I interviewed for, and some of those jobs were not right for me.

If I would have been hired for one of those jobs I interviewed for I would have taken it, and may have had a really terrible time at the job. Since teaching for twenty years I have gotten my administrative endorsement and have tried to be an administrator, but again I have not been offered a job. In a way I am very pleased about this, because I do not have to go through the stress many principals have to go through.

It is not about me. It is about the people around me. It is about the greater good. It is about making a difference. It is about being the best I can be for those around me. It is about looking at life in a different perspective. It is changing my attitude and thought process to be able to make a difference in the lives of others and in the end make my life more meaningful, fun, and joyful.

The Negative

You cannot fully enjoy life if you think of yourself. If you are prideful, arrogant, and selfish things will be really hard for you and find it hard to enjoy all of the experiences in your life. If you find yourself being negative, blaming others for bad things happening to you, and being always worried bad things will happen to you, then it is time to redirect your thought process.

It is important to move past the negative in your life. You need to see yourself as a positive, talented, good natured person who helps others. Sure you have weaknesses, everyone does, but it is time to learn from them and make them strengths. It is time to use your talents to help others. It is time to always be positive and think of others before you think of yourself.

I am Third

My thoughts started to change after reading the book I am Third written by Gale Sayers. I had watched the television movie, "Brian's Song," and thought it was a great story so I read the book. It is a true story about Gale Sayers and his friend Brian Piccolo who dies from cancer. Gale Sayers who was one of the best running backs in the NFL history wrote the book after Brian had died.

The movie was a touching story. I really liked it. But it was the message of the book, I liked the best. Gale said that he had a coach that had a quote that read God is first, family is second, and I am third. Gale adopted that quote and lived by it. I really liked it as well.

In everything we do we should not be first. If you are religious God should always be first. Family should always come before you. I would also add friends and neighbors should also come before you as well. If we thought this way, the troubles of the world would be solved. If you live your life like this you will find more comfort and joy than you have ever experienced before.

Buddhism

I like to learn about different cultures as well as religions. When I first learned about the four noble truths and the path to freedom following the eight fold path, I started to understand more fully that it is not about me. The enlightenment of the Buddha gave us is that suffering in the world comes from our desires and in order to be happy we need to overcome our desires. In other words we need to forget ourselves. It is not about me.

Buddhism also teaches about rebirth. We often think of this as reincarnation. You can look at it as renewing ourselves each day through correction of thought and action. First we change our thinking process so we forget ourselves and second we start to think of others and act upon those thoughts.

Lose Yourself

Jesus Christ taught that we must lose ourselves in order to find ourself. He taught a lot about how we need to think about others and serve others. He asked his disciples to leave their lives and follow him. They gave up their careers to follow him. The message he gave was that of forgiveness and compassion to others.

You have to lose your selfishness, your pride, and your self pity in order to gain the world. Once you are able to do this you are able to truly understand what Jesus taught. He was able to demonstrate this throughout his life as he forgot himself and served those he met.

Chapter Two: Friends

Who are true friends? They are those who do not think about themselves. They are those who think of their friends first. They are those who wish the best for their friends and will be there if their friends need help.

You can tell what a true friend is like by who they think about the most. If they are constantly thinking about themselves they are not true friends. If you have friends that are doing things that can get you in trouble or are things that may hurt you, then you need to find new friends.

I naturally hung out with kids my own age in my neighborhood. I realized that many of these so called friends liked to tease me and did things that made me feel uncomfortable. I made the decision as a teenager to not be with these friends anymore. This made a hug difference as each of them went in different directions some went on a path that led to trouble.

At the time I just did not want to be with those friends anymore, because I did not feel good being around them. Looking back, I realize I did make the right decision. I could have made a better decision by helping some of those friends to choose a more productive path. If I would have thought about them and reached out, I might have made a difference in their lives.

Things I can control

I have learned that there are things I can control and things I cannot. I cannot control other people. No matter how hard I try I cannot change what people do or say. The decision is up to the person. Just like no one can control my thoughts or actions, I cannot control their thoughts or actions.

I can control what I say, what I do, and what I think. I can form an opinion about something. I can control my attitude. I can control how I interact with other people. I can control what I do for my friends. I can control what kind of friend I want to be. I can control my perception on life. It's not about me.

I cannot control what a person thinks about me. I cannot control how that person acts around me. I cannot control if the person likes me or not. I cannot control the person's attitude or opinion about something. I cannot control the path a person chooses.

I can just control what I do and it is what I do that can make all of the difference. We do not have to worry about other people's actions as much as we do our own. By doing our part we can influence what other people do and say. Eventually our actions can cause a chain reaction that brings about a marvelous change.

Left Behind

I remember standing in line waiting to be picked to be on a team to play a game. I was often one of the last to be picked and there were a couple of times I was left behind and not picked to play in the game. This can be very painful as a kid to think that no one wants you to play with them. The hardest part to all of this was that I was an okay athlete, but a lot of kids and coaches did not give me a chance. I was often one of the shortest in my grade, so everyone assumed that I was not very good at sports. My self esteem didn't help much.

There were kids that were not very good at sports, but they were outgoing so they got noticed by others. I had learned that those who are loud are often heard above the crowd and get noticed. I was the quiet shy kid who often had his head down. It wasn't any wonder I did not get noticed.

I was often left behind in just about everything, unnoticed unless I was the target of being bullied. This fueled my depression and the withdrawal from society. I was thinking about myself. I ended up with few friends, or so I thought. It is interesting how we tend to perceive what is happening in our lives. I assumed I didn't have too many friends and many people either did not like me or didn't know I existed.

The major problem was that I did withdraw from just about everything which eliminated personal contact. So I may have had friends, but I was the one who withdrew from them. I did not reach out to those around me. I did not seek out new friends. I did not open my eyes and notice other children around me who may have been feeling left out as well. I was so self absorbed that I did not notice anyone else.

There were a few friends I did managed to talk with at school through the years, but I did not reach out to get any closer than that. It wasn't until my family moved to Ohio my sophomore year in high school that I suddenly had some friends to hang out with.

I felt very much along moving to Ohio with my family and did not know anyone. The high school I went to was big and scary with big and scary kids walking around. I returned to my old ways and did not reach out to make any new friends. There were a few friends that I had got to know in my classes, but that was about it.

The place I had gotten to know more friends was at church. I am a Mormon and in Ohio I was definitely a minority. So when I went to church and found several kids my age we instantly were friends. Only a few of them went to the school I went to. We grew our friendship through church and church activities. It was a strange feeling for me to instantly have girls come up to me and be friendly. I was a little overwhelmed by this. There were several girls and a couple of boys who were around my age. I was able to become friends with each of them.

I made the mistake of thinking about myself again and got depressed that some of the girls didn't not want to become my girlfriend. I think it is so much a guy thing. If I would have only known what I know now. It wasn't that they thought I was ugly or a jerk. It was just that they were young and didn't want to get serious with anyone. It was a good think too.

There are so many kids these days who get serious way to young and end up with problems. If you think about the other person and your friends you would not ask them to do something they are no willing to do or something that would hurt them. I was fortunate that I did not get involved when I was young.

I could have thought more about those who were my friends and came up with ways to have helped them. I could have thought of small and simple ways to have involved them in my life and made them feel good.

Never leave anyone out of things. Seek those who are alone and involve them in your life. Some of your best friends will be the ones who are sitting alone during lunch or are the ones chosen last to be

20

on a team. These are often the ones who become really successful in life and they will put you on the right path in life. Do not follow the crowd. It is often the wrong path you want to go. Remember to follow the crowd you are thinking of yourself. It's not about me. Follow those who are unique and interesting in their own right. The Einsteins and Edisons both who were left behind in school and among their peers.

Friend to All

Do not exclude yourself from the friendship of others. Even if someone is the total opposite of you and it is hard to be in their presence you can still be her friend. You may learn some vital lessons from her. You may just learn that you do not like it when a person is negative, swears a lot, and wears trashy clothes. You may learn what not to do from people, by simply being their friend.

I had a couple of friends in high school and I just happened to fall into for some strange reason. I don't remember how I started to hang out with them during lunch, but somehow it did. It was a very odd situation and we were an odd group. I don't even know if this impacted what other kids thought of me at the time either.

I was with this large guy and his girlfriend who was also large as girls go. Both of them were friendly enough, but did not share the same values as I did. They were the type to skip class, go to parties, drink alcohol, and maybe even do drugs. I am not even sure if they graduated from high school. I just remember being with them. It was almost as if I was some sort of support to them. They did in a strange way give support to me as well.

I did not make the same mistakes as they did. One day during lunch they bought some wine coolers and spiked their soft drinks with them. They offered me a drink, but I turned them down. I did not participate in what they did, but the neat thing about our relationship was that they did not tease me or judge me and I didn't tease or judge them.

The key to being a friend to others is not to judge them. It is okay to point out things they may be doing wrong and try to steer them on the right path in life. Friends do things to help others, but do not judge them or anyone else for what they do. This brings down all of the barriers when it comes to having friends. You never know when a person who befriend becomes a very influential person in your life.

I like how in Scotland people say, "Sorry, and No Worries," a lot when it comes to making a mistake or when someone else makes a mistake. It says a lot about how friendly the atmosphere is in Scotland. They own up to their mistakes and do not judge others for their mistakes.

Chapter Three: Family

It's not about me, it's about my family. Most people would agree that their family comes first. One of the first things my principal said to the faculty the first week we came back from the summer was that family comes first.

Everything you do should have your family in mind. It is not about you, it is about your family, your future family, and your extended family. You will never know when you will be called up to help your parents, siblings, a nephew, or a grandparent. You may not know the true influence of your actions on future grandchildren.

Just think about how the action of one person has impacted their children, their grandchildren, and their great grandchildren. Poverty is a generational thing which is passed on. It is the same for abuse and poor health. It only takes one person to change all of this for the next generation.

If you were to just look at family histories and how the generations played out, you can identify the direction the family went by the decision of a single individual. Just think about the man who decided to travel across the ocean to be in America in 1791. He meets a woman here and they get married and have children. They start their own business and work hard to be successful. Their children all go through school and become successful. Soon there is a generation of successful people as the result of the one person coming to America.

Some of the most successful people in history came to America and worked from rags to riches. Their children lives in wealth instead of poverty and their children's children are highly educated and skilled.

Generations

Think about how your actions will impact your children and grandchildren. If you knew your children would follow in your footsteps and do everything you did, would you take drugs, commit crimes, and make stupid mistakes that harm others. This is what has happened to countless people sending a ripple effect through generations.

How do your children see you? Do they think of you as their hero? Do they want to be just like you? Are they scared of you? Do they hate you? Do they want to hide when you come out to see their friends?

Measure of a Man

The measure of a man is how well he takes care of his family. I knew of a young man who spend a lot of time with friends and doing things he liked to do instead of spending it with his family. He rarely came to family events and took a lot of vacations away from his family to spend it with his friends. The end result of this was that he lost his family. The marriage ended up in divorce, and he saw his children part time. The marriage would have been saved if he would have thought of his family first instead of himself.

Time will only tell what happens to this man's children as the result of his selfishness. The interesting thing about this story is that the man didn't commit any crime, he did not do drugs, and was a very nice guy. He was willing to help others and was great around his kids. Just the fact he did not take the time to spend precious moments with his family was a key factor in the breakup.

There are so many things these days that take us from our families. There is work, school, personal interests, and our friends. The trick is to find a way to combine some of these things and think of ways to include your family in your life. There are families that work together in a family business. There are families that become close with other families and they do activities together and take vacations together. You can include your family in some of your hobbies or interests.

Each summer we get together with my wife's friend's family and take a vacation together. We often share our interests with each other and come up with common things to do with each other like go see a play or movie with each other. We also enjoy taking walks and hikes with each other.

It is often the small and simple things we think of doing for our families that matters the most. It could be a loving text or email. It could be bringing home some flowers, or it could be having dinner together as a family.

I try to have dinner as a family and pray together as a family every day. We also try to do an activity once a week as a family. We attend church each week as a family. We check with each other on a daily basis and get involved with each others work and school activities.

The best part of my day is to come home and be with my family. It is also when I am thinking of my family and not of myself. I love my family and know that they love me, there isn't anything better than this.

Chapter Four: Community

"...Ask not what your country can do for you, ask what you can do for your country..."

John F. Kennedy

We live in an age of government handouts. People expect the government to give them a lot and in return not to take anything from them. This makes for a very weak society where people are not willing to do their part in making the community strong. There is a difference between a community where everyone hides in their homes and does not think about making their community better, and a community where everyone is working together to improve their community.

When I lived in Chicago, it was difficult to find a sense of community in some places, because of the amount of people living in an area. There were little pockets here and there where the people were bonded by family and ethnic backgrounds. Some of these communities were very close and many of the people knew each other and everything that happened in the community. This was in 1987 a time when most people did not have cell phones, and smart phones didn't exist. It was a time when the home computer did very little and only a handful of people owned them.

Now even in many of the small communities, people spend their time with there heads down looking at their phones. People spend a lot of screen time each day and very little time out in the community seeing people face-to-face. The sense of community has changed.

When I was a child the kids in the neighborhood were always outside playing. Now it is hard to notice anyone outside unless they are doing yard work or doing their daily walk or jog. We do not get out like people used to. There is less social interaction. In a way this has brought down people's sense of community involvement, and their sense of thinking about their community.

If something bad happens communities will be suddenly awakened to it. There was a bad accident in my neighborhood involving some children. They were all on a small motor cart that overturned. None of them were wearing helmets or seatbelt and the driver was underage. People may have wondered why the parents allowed this.

The tragic part of this story was that no one in the neighborhood attempted to prevent this accident. The children had been riding around like this for several weeks before the accident. I even saw the kids and thought that it was safe, but I did not do anything about it. Just a kind reminder to the children or the parents may have prevented the accident.

There is a saying that it takes a village to raise a child. This is so true. Parents are important in the process of raising a child, but it is who the child interacts with that is important. This is often the children in their neighborhood and those children's parents.

Church

A church in an area can bring a good sense of community to the area. It brings people together, and helps in many ways through service to the community. Many of the things involving the

28

members of the church receive the support of its members.

I have always gone to church and have found a strong sense of community with the church I go to. At church the members come together through service and fellowship. Many of the members take the extra time to think of others in the church and seek to take care of each other.

The church is split up into wards that are often small community areas where members of the church not only look after each other, they look after everyone within the boundaries of the ward. When there might be a disaster in the area it is the church that is organized enough to be able to offer aid almost immediately.

The way the church is organized and how its members work together is what a true community should be like. It is the essence of making a community work.

Civic Duty

"The only thing necessary for the triumph of evil is for good men to do nothing."

Edmund Burke

Hitler and the Nazis were elected into the German government by the people. It was the people who allowed Hitler to become absolute leader, to start World War II and to allow the Holocaust to happen. Finally it was the allied forces that stopped Hitler and brought an end to the Holocaust.

Ronald Reagan and Mikhail Gorbachev worked together to end the cold war and to take down the Berlin wall. These two great leaders were able to reshape the modern world. A lot of people now have freedom because of their efforts.

It is our duty to be involved with local and national politics in order to ensure we have the best people in office. It may be difficult to vote sometimes when there is not as many good candidates running, but it is important to be able to be involved in what is happening. It is important to know what laws are being made or changed and to voice your opinion for the common good of your community.

Unfortunately there are some people in it for themselves and their friends. They may be passing laws that are not in the best interest of the community, because it is in favor of their friends. It is the duty of every citizen to make sure to remind our representatives that they need to serve the community and not special interests of others.

Be the Change

If you want to be able to have a good community you need to help bring about the change for a better tomorrow. It's not about you, it's about making a good community for the next generation. The future can be hard with a lot of challenges, but it can be a lot brighter with the hope of creating an environment of trust and love for each other.

Chapter Five: Work

It is too easy to blame all of our problems on how stressful work is. You probably have come home some days and vented your frustration how your boss is an idiot or you do not like working with someone. You may complain about how tired you are and you are being overworked. You may complain that you are not appreciated or never get credit for your hard work. In some ways your feelings have some basis in fact. But you are looking at it from your point of view. You are thinking about yourself when it comes to work.

Now lets change things around and look at your job through the eyes of your boss, the eyes of a co-worker, or your clients. Then change your attitude to a positive one. Thing about forgiving those who may have hurt you. Letting go of all of the stress that comes from work, and then start thinking about others. Remember it is not about you. Most business are about the customers.

In education it is all about the students. We are attempting to make the best students we can so they can learn to be productive citizens and to give something back to society after they graduate from high school and college. This is the hope and goal of education. Then why do teachers come away thinking about themselves? Because they are human like the rest of the people in the world and naturally start to think about teaching as something to provide for themselves and their families.

A good teacher may think about her students, a poor teacher will think about herself and what she needs to do to make the most out of teaching instead of making the most out of helping her students. I have struggled in my teaching career to stay balanced between being a devoted teacher to my students and spending my other time with family and other areas of my life.

The Boss

A good supervisor, manager, or CEO of a company will not think of herself, but that of her employees and the good of the company. She would get to know her employees and what their weaknesses and strengths were. She would use every available resource to help benefit the company. She would be able to find ways to rewards her employees for their hard work.

I have had several bosses over the years as I worked my way through college, worked after graduating from college between getting into teaching, and then having several principals at each school I have worked at. I have even had five principals over the past nine years at the current school I work at.

I would have to say the best boss I have had was when I was working at a university as a custodian. My supervisor was very personable and thought of the people he supervised. He would have a luncheon every other Friday for the crew and let us leave early every other Friday. He worked with me as I took college classes to change my work schedule. He allowed me to use my sick leave to find a place to live when I got a teaching job. He even took me out to lunch at a restaurant the last week I was on the job.

I really liked the job, despite the fact I was getting paid just a little above minimum wage. It was a great job since I had virtually no stress and the work was not very difficult to do. It was my boss who made the job worth while.

There have been principals I have likes and some who I did not get along with as much. The difference was those who showed that they cared and thought of their employees. I have often questioned why some of the people were chosen in the positions they were placed in. I may never know for sure, but it did not seem like they were chosen because they were the best fit for the position.

I have often questioned the direction or actions of administration at the schools I have worked at. The trap I believe a lot of people get into when it comes to school principals is that they get into a negative loop where they blame everything on the principals and do not see the whole picture. There are so many factors when it comes to running a school that it takes a team effort to make it happen.

There was a time when I was placed in a position where I was dealing with students that misbehaved in the school. It became a very stressful and difficult position to handle. I was given two staff assistants to help me, but I never was able to figure out how to use them effectively.

I was often doing ten things at a time. I ran lunch detention, in-school suspension, and was monitoring hallways and lunches. I was keeping track of students who were late to class. I was even trying to come up with reward incentives for the teachers and the students of the school. I ran a school store out of my classroom where students could come and buy snacks and other items. It was a crazy time dealing with all of the things that year. On top of all these things I was also teaching an honors geography class one day and a criminal justice class the next day. My criminal justice class was also doing youth court with students who had done some misbehaviors.

I felt bad that the principal told me I would not be doing it the next year. But it ended up being a blessing to have taken a break from doing it. I went back to teaching for a year, and then went back to running the detention room and in-school suspension for another two years. It was hard when I did this because I lost my lunch and any restroom breaks during the day. I had to dehydrate myself in order to get through the day. By the end of the day I was dizzy and had a headache.

The lesson I learned was that I constantly thought about what I could do to impress people by working hard and trying to accomplish everything. If there was a problem during lunch I did everything I could to solve the problem. If there was a need I tried to fill it. This was all good in my mind. Yet I never got the recognition for it or any type of reward. This embittered me as I tried to understand why no one saw how hard of a worker I was and all of the things I had done.

It was not about me. It was about working with others and getting the buy in from others to make things work. I realized that I could not do everything and I really did need help from others in order to solve problems. True leaders are not the ones who do all of the work, but encourage and manage to get others to do the work.

I have found the same thing in my classroom. If I just stand up in front of the class and lecture, or try to do everything in the class, I have a hard time with my students. Yet if I involve the students and have them do most of the work it is better for both my students and myself.

When I was in a position of leadership, I should have thought of others and tried to find ways to include them in what needed to be done. It is really hard for people to be able to truly fit in at work unless they feel like they are needed and appreciated.

Coworkers

It can be unbearable sometimes to work with people. We come to work with our own personalities, biases, and the way we do things. This often clashes with those we work with. It can be difficult to be able to understand where someone is coming from when they do things. Imagine being thrown into a room with complete strangers and told that each of you had to work as a team to accomplish a task. This is often the scenario at work.

There may be times when the people are able to get along well together, and then there are times when they constantly argue with each other. It is almost like flipping a coin when it comes to work relationships. The biggest problem comes from pride and ego. There will be those who will have an opinion and will not relent. Their way is the best way and everyone should agree.

I have found again that it is not about me. It's about what is best for the students. If I disagree with a teacher in the school I first need to think about what is best for the students, and then I think about what the other teacher's point of view is. I am then able to be able to express my feelings to the other teacher. In most cases this scenario works out. The objective would be to work together as a team to be able to help the students of the school.

It doesn't make the job any less stressful to be negative to your coworkers. It can make the job more enjoyable if you are able to think about your coworkers and come up with ways to get along with them. You would also need to keep your customers or clients in mind as you make changes and work along side other people who may start out as strangers, but end up as friends.

The Customers

Successful businesses have great customer service. The customer is always right is the motto of many businesses. They put the customer first and think of ways to please the customer. Many businesses have customers fill out surveys to let them know what they could do better. Without the customers the business would go out of business.

In teaching it is the students that are the customers. If it wasn't for the students I would not have a job. I lost my first teaching job, because there was a reduction in force due to the drop in enrollment. I have complained about having large classes with 45 students in my classroom, but I realize it is not about me it is about the students and without them I would not be there. So I don't worry about the size of the class as much because I know I will always have a job if my class sized are large.

There are some days when I feel like throwing a student out the door and telling them not to ever come back. Then I think about how I have an ethic to do what I can to help this student and to attempt to teach the student. It is my job to serve every student I am given to teach. I must do what I can to help them to learn the material I am told to teach from my administrator.

I know that I cannot force students to learn the material and they have the choice to do what I ask or not. I still need to do what I can to reach each student and do what I can to help them. It's not about me, it's about each student I see.

Chapter Six: Jesus Christ

"For whosoever will save his life shall lose it: but whosoever will lose his life for my sake, the same shall save it."

St. Luke 9:24

Jesus taught by example. He frequently did things for others as his thoughts constantly turned to others. He taught his disciples his ways, blessed those who were sick, and even attempted to explain to those who wished his ill fate their errors. Jesus throughout his mission and his life never thought about himself. He sealed this with his life on the cross in which he freely gave his life. At any moment in Jesus's life he could have chose to not fulfill his mission.

Jesus could have lives a normal life as a carpenter. He could have remained in Egypt when his parents took him there to escape the sword of Herod's wrath. He could have left the area and lived a long happy life just about anywhere. Jesus could have simply not made waves by healthy people or teaching about peace and loving his enemies.

He was the opposite of what the Jewish leadership were looking for in a redeemer. They wanted someone to throw down the Roman army and bring about political power to the Jewish leadership. There was a lot of pride and selfish desire the Jewish were seeking. This is one reason why they sought the life of Jesus who threatened their plans to remain in power over the people.

Jesus gave hls message of selflessness through parables. If you look at the main message in his parables they place an emphasis on thinking of others and not of yourself.

The Prodigal Son (Luke 15: 11-32)

There was a father who had two sons. One of his sons decided to take his inheritance and to waste it on crazy behavior. The son thought nothing but himself. In the end he was eating among the swine. He could not have gotten any lower. The son finally realized what he had done and returned home, not to ask his father for more money, but to ask for a job so he could live like a servant to his father.

The father was so delighted to see his son back decided to have a party for his son. The brother seeing what happened got envious and complained to his father. He wondered why his father never threw a party for him. The father explained to his faithful son that he was always with him and had all that his father had, but his brother was lost and now he was back.

The prodigal son finally realized his folly in thinking about himself. He changed his ways and first thought of his father and working to serve him. His father had never stopped thinking about his son. His faithful son did remain and worked with his father, but had momentarily forgotten this when he became jealous of his brother.

The parable is a great lesson about what happens when you just think about yourself. It also is a lesson of what happens when you think of others. I also like it because it is a classic example of what often happens in families where the children become disobedient and want to leave home and ignore their parents advice.

The Good Samaritan (Luke 10:25-37)

A Lawyer came to Jesus and asked him what he needed to do to inherit eternal life. Jesus answered that he needed to love God and love his neighbor. This Jesus had taught was the two great commandments. He had taught about loving others throughout his ministry.

The lawyer then asked who is his neighbor. Jesus answered with the parable of the good Samaritan. He told of a man who was robbed and beaten. The man needed help, but two people of high standing in the community passed without helping him thinking only of themselves. The third man was a Samaritan who was despised by the Jews. He stopped and helped the man. Jesus then asked the lawyer which man was a neighbor to the man who had fallen among the thieves?

The lawyer said that it was the man who showed mercy to the injured man. Jesus then told him to do the same. The message was clear we need to be like the good Samaritan and help our neighbor. The neighbor is anyone who may need our help.

Sermon on the mount (Matthew chapters 5,6, and 7)

The sermon on the mount given by Jesus was when he spoke to a large gathering of people. His message was simple. People need to think of others. He talked of those who were humble and charitable as the ones who would inherit the kingdom of God. He expanded upon the Ten Commandments to include thoughts. If a person thinks evil thoughts he has committed sin in his heart.

This is an important lesson about human nature. People will first think about a crime in their mind and then carry it out in their actions. It is only when we recognize that these evil thoughts in our mind and get rid of them we can control our actions. If we think of ourselves we will do selfish things. If we think evil of others we will do evil things to others.

It is only when we start to think that it is not about us, that we truly understand Christ's message. We need to reprogram our minds as we go about our daily routines to think of others.

The Atonement (Luke 22)

Jesus met with his disciples for the last supper. He told them several things. They wanted to know which of them would be the greatest. He explained that it was the one who was the least who served the others. He had identified Judas who was about to betray him.

Judas had been steeling money from the donations they had received and was going to betray Christ for money. He was not thinking about his master, but himself and the promise of wealth.

Jesus told Peter that he would deny him three times. He was at the last moment teaching Peter a valuable lesson about humility. Peter was not the man he needed to be yet. He still was selfish enough to deny knowing Jesus to save his own life. Peter learned his lesson and became more committed after he realized what he had done by denying he knew Jesus.

Jesus went to Gathsemane to pay for the sins of the world. He knew it was going to be difficult, even for a man who was part god. He asked if he could be spared this, but was willing to do what he was asked to do of the Father. He was again thinking of his Father and of each of us.

The Cross (Matthew 27, John 19)

After spending the night suffering for the sins of the world Jesus was betrayed by a kiss and taken to an unlawful court to be mocked and scourged. He endured all of this as he thought about the people and not himself. He could have stopped this at any point, but he volunteered to endure all of it to the end.

Jesus was still thinking of others as he was looking down from the cross. He told John to take care of his mother. He told one of the thieves that he was see him in paradise. He forgave the Roman soldiers for their part in his crucification. His act of selfless sacrifice was a model for everyone to follow.

Even if you are not a Christian or do not believe in God, you can learn from Christ's example as he constantly thought about other people and willingly gave up his life for everyone even those who do wickedly.

Accepting Christ

My intent is not to convert you or make you believe enough to be a Christian or join a particular church. The intent is to understand Christ's message and to accept his message. This comes from fully understanding the power of the message. Many religions around the world teach the same message in their own way.

The message is simple. Love your neighbor as yourself. Give up your thoughts of becoming rich and famous. Turn your thoughts toward the compassion and love for other people including those you do not know. It is only when you do this you will be able to see a wonderful change in your life.

Chapter Seven: A Mighty Change (Attitude)

Change must first come from within, before it can happen without. You cannot see any real changes in your life until you first change the way you think and the thoughts you allow to dwell in your mind. You cannot simply think of a couple of nice things you can do for someone you are about. It needs to be a mighty change a largest enough change to make a real impact on your life.

People every year go through the routine of losing weight to feel better about themselves. Many struggle to lose any weight while others are able to lose a lot of weight in a matter of only a few weeks. They are pleased with themselves for their accomplishment and then they start to gain the weight back again.

This yo-yo dieting is very common and most people go through it at one point in their lives. The problem is that their is no real change taking place in their minds about losing weight. They think it is simply the idea of losing the weight and don't realize they need to change the way they are thinking, their attitude about things, and their lifestyle. It has to be a more complete change a mighty change for it to take hold and be more permanent.

A yo-yo dieter will just think about cutting back on eating and doing some exercise until he loses the weight. Then after losing the weight he will reward himself by eating some dessert. He hasn't really changed the way he feels about food and his eating habits. So he goes back to his former routine and gains the weight back.

A lifestyle change will make the lost weight more permanent. This requires a change in attitude and thoughts about eating. He thinks about eating healthy foods and eating less of it. He changes his lifestyle by making a habit of exercise and buying only healthy foods. Their is nothing in his mind about eating junk food, in fact he learns to despise it. The thought of eating at a fast food restaurant makes him feel sick. His underlining thoughts are that he needs to be healthy in order to be their for his family and friends.

Thinking of others is a great foundation for a healthy lifestyle change. When you do things for others you tend to be more motivated for the long term than if you were motivated for yourself. A person who runs the race for himself will reach the finish line and find himself all alone. A person who runs the race for others will have those people waiting for him when he finishes the race.

Attitude

Attitude is the one thing you can control in your life and has a profound impact on you and those around you. No one can make you have an attitude. You make the choice everyday what attitude you are going to carry around with you for the rest of the day. There have been countless people who have gone through terrible events and still maintained a positive attitude. Then there are those who carry a negative attitude with them despite having a wonderful life.

The attitude I carry with me determines what kind of experience I will have. If I have a bad attitude no matter how positive the experience is, I will have a bad time of it. If I have a positive attitude no matter how awful the experience is I will survive it with a smile on my face. It is truly amazing how much power

your attitude really has on the experiences you face
in your life.

Thoughts

Thoughts come from the emotions and
stimulus you have as you go through experiences. If
you are robbed you will feel scared, upset, and mad.
You may think about it happening again. You may
reply it over and over again in your mind. You may
think about how you are going to buy a gun and not
let it happen to you again. You may feel like you are a
loser and bad things always happen to you. You may
feel helpless and weak.

Lets take the same experience of being
robbed and change the thoughts. You can think
about why the people robbed you. Maybe they were
desperate and needed money for medicine for
someone who is dying. They may have had a rough
childhood and robbing people is one of the only
things they know. This could be the first time they did
this and are just as scared as you are and didn't really
want to do it.

Maybe they are really just evil to the core, but
do you want to carry the baggage with you for what
they did to you. The victims of crimes often suffer for
years not physically, but emotionally as they will not
forgive or forget what happened. They hold on to
having been violated and will not move on in their
lives. With an attitude of forgiveness and working to
move on and letting go of the experience you are
able to take control of your life again and not allow
the experience to rule your life.

It is really about attitude and how this rules
your life. You can choose to have a poor attitude and

be miserable for the rest of your life, or you can choose to have a more positive attitude and be able to have a great time throughout your life. It is not about me, it is about having a positive attitude with others in mind.

Lifestyle

A mighty change only takes place when there is a change in lifestyle. An alcoholic cannot stay sober living with her friends who are constantly drinking and offering her drinks. She would eventually give in to the temptations of her friends. This is one reason why people who are addicted to drugs have such a hard time breaking the habit. They are often surrounded by other people who are addicted and end up feeding on each others desires for the next hit or drink.

Successful recovering addicts are those who make a lifestyle change and hang around people who do not drink or do drugs. They remove themselves from the temptations of going to restaurants with bars, stop going to parties with drugs, and choose to replace this with other interests.

The key to a lifestyle change is to eliminate the negative and replace it with the positive. Once the positive is entrenched in your life you will not have a desire to go back to the way you were living before. A lifestyle change is a mighty change that can have a dramatic impact on your life.

The lifestyle change for the better would involve seeking ways to think about others and do things with others in mind. This would involve being service oriented. You walk up to a door and you hold it open for someone next to you. Someone drops something on the floor and you pick it up for them. You change your thinking to serving others. There will be amazing opportunities for you to be there when someone needs your help. The great thing about this is that you will feel so much better about your life. You will feel happier, feel more energetic, and better things will start to happen in your life.

Chapter Eight: Full Circle

Rugged individualism and the American dream bring images of a person working her way to the top from poverty. It has been the ideal America has been founded upon. It is also only part of the story. It doesn't tell about all of the American Indians who were slaughtered to make way for someone else to take their land. It doesn't talk about the thousands of people who have been discriminated for their religious beliefs, their former nationality, and their race. It doesn't bring into the light the millions of people brought to America in bondage from Africa to work on plantations so people could become rich.

America has come a long way since its beginning. It has grown to be a nation where people come for a new life of freedom. There are a lot of opportunities, and yes there is still the American dream of freedom, of getting into a career of your choice, of owning a home, and raising a family. Yet in America it is still about the individual.

Schools teach to the students they need to be successful if they get good grades and go through the hoops of society. They teach students to be hard working and to make the best of themselves. This of course works for some and there are those who are able to realize it is not all about them. But I cannot help think that society is teaching the next generation to be selfish and arrogant in achieving success. It is all about the individual, sure there is the nationalism thing, but even this is shrouded in selfishness and not accepting other nations of the earth as equals.

There is hints of compassion towards others. People do help others through selfless acts of service and kindness. There is millions of dollars given to charities, and many people spend countless hours in the service to others.

But I can't help thinking about how many programs on television focusing on the individual. Movies focusing on the person who is selfish being successful. The super hero movies where the super hero has all of this cool things he can do. Yes the super hero saves the day by helping people, and serves the community. But is this the real message of the movie, perhaps, but children are not excited about helping people. They are excited about dressing up as a super hero and pretending to have some really cool powers.

The Cool Kids

In school the most popular kids in the school are the jocks, the cheerleaders, and the rich kids who dress really fancy. They form the cool kids clicks. Many of the students in the school dream to be just like these other students. Many of them are filled up with how wonderful they are and all of the neat things they can do.

Then there are the gangsters or troublemakers who attempt to rebel at everything. They feel like they can never be like the cool kids in the school so they choose to be the opposite. These students do everything in their power to defy the authority of the school so in their own eyes they are the cool kids. There are a number of students who want to be like these kids and they do not have to be a good athlete, cheerleader, smart, or rich to join. They just need to do rotten things and get treated like crap by the rest of the gangsters.

There are the nerds trying desperately to get scholarships to college so they can redeem themselves from being the nerds in school. They get good grades and spend their time with their heads in books. Many of them like to be on computers as well.

Growing up I desperately wanted to be apart of a click in school. I tried the jock thing, but really didn't get noticed by the coaches to have much playing time, and no one else in the school really noticed me either. I didn't work hard enough to get good enough grades to get on the honor role. My family was not rich enough to buy me fancy clothes. I did not want to belong to the gangsters. I really thought that drugs and the violence thing was stupid.

So I was left alone without belonging to any click at school. In a way I was part of the out castes in school. The group that really did not belong with any other group and no one knew existed. The strange thing was that I had the same sense of individualism and sense of being the best I could be for my own selfish reasons as just about everyone else in those clicks.

For some magical reason there are those who find the path that leads to altruism. They finally realize it is not about them. They understand that true happiness comes from serving others and being the best they can to help others. The students who are in this group do not get glamorized and are not part of the popular kids in school. They are under the radar of most of the student body.

Rich and Famous

The temptation of wanting to be rich and famous is very strong throughout the world and even stronger in the United States. It is what most children seek as they go through school. There heroes are the athletes that make millions of dollars each year. They also have heroes who are in the movies or who are in bands. You ask who children admire the most or who their heroes are and many of them will mention someone who is famous or rich.

I was the typical American boy who wanted to be a professional football player. I wanted to be a professional singer. I wanted to be an actor. I wanted to be rich and famous like many of the people I saw while growing up that I admired at the time. I wanted to be like many of the people I saw on the movies. I liked several athletes and actors. They were my role models.

It wasn't until I became an adult how flawed me thinking was. I was admiring the wrong people. The movie stars and athletes I admired were not going to teach me anything that was of benefit in my life except to be selfish and to hurt other people in order to become rich and famous.

There is a price for everything. In many cases the price for wealth and fame is loneliness and sadness. This is why you see many of the rich and famous going from one relationship to the next. They have just as many problems as everyone else in their lives and they are less happy for it.

I should not discount everyone who has money and fame. There are many who are very compassionate giving people who share their wealth with the less fortunate. There are those who are kind loving people.

On the road to wealth and fame it is often the case that people become selfish and start to do things that hurt the people around them. It may not be the road that changes them, it could be the wealth and fame that turns a person into a monster.

I had gotten an audiobook about Elvis Presley. It was released audio recordings of him talking to people. When he first was becoming famous he was a very pleasant person who was very personable. From the other things I read about him, Elvis was a very polite well mannered young man. Then after his wealth and fame he began to change. The later tapes revealed a very different person. It revealed a selfish angry spiteful person. This confirms what happened to him the last years of his life.

My heroes now are those who have made a difference in the world through selfless acts of kindness and a determination to help others. The first is my father who taught me to have integrity. He also taught me to get involved in service. I also have many religious heroes who have taught me the true meaning of giving oneself to help those in need. I would also include people like Gandhi who taught the world the true meaning of non-violence and love for others. There are so many that I could put in my personal hall-of-fame that I may write a book about them.

Journey

There is a journey each of us take through life. We learn a lot along the way. It is our choices in our journey through life that allows us to learn and grow from the experiences that are placed in front of us. We gain opportunities through these choices and find happiness or sorrow, love or hate, compassion or selfish desire. What happens in life is up to us. It is not about what happens to us, nor is it our circumstances, it is about what we do for others.

It is not about me. It is about what I make of myself for the benefit of others. It is about how I treat my family. It is about what I can contribute to my community. It is about how I can impact the lives of the students I teach. It is about the love and joy I receive through service. It is about being motivated to do things as I think of others.

I have spent most of my life thinking about me, now is the time I change this way of thinking and start thinking about others. It is a time for me to change my path in life and to focus on the good things. It is about seeking to do the small things for those who need someone to help them on the right path.

Karma

The strange thing is that when you start to think about others and not make your life about you, great things start to happen in your life. You become happier, full of life, have more friends, get closer to your family, and several opportunities come your way. This is often known as karma. What you do will come back to you. You complete a full circle when you make life about other people. Your single act of kindness, your thoughts of others, and your selfless attitude will come back to you ten fold.

In other words, if everyone thought of others, there is someone right now thinking of you right now. It is about me and it is about you.

Printed in Poland
by Amazon Fulfillment
Poland Sp. z o.o., Wrocław